Cautionary Tales

Young people, crime and policing in Edinburgh

SIMON ANDERSON
RICHARD KINSEY
IAN LOADER
CONNIE SMITH

Avebury

Aldershot · Brookfield USA · Hong Kong · Singapore · Sydney

Published by
Avebury
Ashgate Publishing Limited
Gower House
Croft Road
Aldershot
Hants GU11 3HR
England

Ashgate Publishing Company
Old Post Road
Brookfield
Vermont 05036
USA

British Library Cataloguing in Publication Data

Anderson, Simon
    Cautionary Tales: Young People, Crime and
    Policing in Edinburgh
    I. Title
    364.36094134
 ISBN 1 85628 851 X

Library of Congress Cataloging-in-Publication Data

Cautionary tales: young people, crime and policing in
    Edinburgh / Simon Anderson ... [et al.]
       p. cm.
    Includes bibliographical references.
    ISBN 1-85628-851-X : $55.95 (est.)
    1.Juvenile delinquency--Scotland--Edinburgh. 2. Youth--
    Scotland--Edinburgh--Social conditions. 3. Victims of crime--
    Scotland--Edinburgh. 4. Crime--Scotland--Edinburgh.
    I. Anderson, Simon, 1965- .
    HV9147.E35C38 1994
    364.3'6'094134--dc20
                                                    94-18854
                                                       CIP

Printed and Bound in Great Britain by
Athenaeum Press Ltd, Newcastle upon Tyne.

Contents

List of figures

CHAPTER 3

CHAPTER 4

CHAPTER 5

List of tables

Acknowledgements

From the time of its inception back in the summer of 1988 this project benefited from the assistance of a great many people. First and foremost our thanks go to Lothian Regional Council for commissioning the research in the first place. Particular thanks in this regard are due to Councillors Paul Nolan, Elizabeth Maginnis and former Councillor Annette Lamont, and to Russell Forrest in the Education Department. Equally importantly, we must thank the headteachers of the schools for allowing us access, and the teachers who both tolerated our presence and ensured the research progressed smoothly and enjoyably.

In addition, our thanks go to Caroline Grove Smith and Jeremy Wood for their work on both the survey and interviews. We also owe an immense debt of gratitude to Toby Morris, Christine Reece, Frances Proven and Gillian Kirkwood at the University of Edinburgh Computing Service for their unstinting help when the computers baffled us. We are also grateful to Ian Dunn for sharing with us his encyclopaedic knowledge of Edinburgh and its history, and to Ed Smith for his enthusiasm. Thanks also to members of the Centre for Criminology and the Social and Philosophical Study of Law at the University of Edinburgh and to all those people who have commented on our work during the various seminars we have given in the last couple of years.

Finally, of course, our thanks are due to the young people who completed the survey and took part in the interviews.

We gratefully acknowledge the permission of Hutchinson and Co (Publishers) Ltd to reproduce material from Cliff Hague's (1984) *The Development of Planning Thought*, and of Penguin Books Ltd to reproduce material from Phillippe Aries' (1962) *Centuries of Childhood*.

Foreword

Throughout its history, British criminology's curiosity with regard to the young has almost exclusively been restricted to the identification and correction of the young male delinquent. In this respect, of course, criminology has faithfully reflected the equally narrow interests of the culture; in Britain - this old and settled society - young people seem ever and always to have been a source of anxiety and trouble. They are - as Stanley Cohen (1972) pointed out some time ago - 'a metaphor for social change' - and often, especially when new youth cultural styles have begun to emerge, an angry metaphor for changes which that comfortable, socially powerful and adult fraction of English society had generally not wanted or even positively resented.

At several points during the late nineteenth and twentieth centuries groups of young men have been constructed as the feared Other in society, viewed as symbols of a breakdown of community and trust, or even, in some accounts, as the source of such a breakdown. In the post-war period, a never-ending sequence of youthful 'folk-devils' (teddy boys, mods and rockers, skinheads, football hooligans) have been paraded through the media and the popular imagination.

In the meantime, official criminology's cold and formal models of delinquency have come to be mirrored in fictional accounts - for example, in the novels of disenchanted emigres like Anthony Burgess in the *Clockwork Orange* and William Golding in *The Lord of the Flies* - as well as in the continuing shock and horror stories of the popular press about 'gangs' and 'yobbos' on the street. There is a strong sense of a society - or at least a network of fictions writers, journalists and academic commentators - that really does not like young people very much, especially when they are the offspring of the lower orders.

The contrast, as so often in matters criminological, is with the United States. For all that America has always had a higher rate of crime than Britain, especially among the young, it has also consistently generated what we might call a sympathetic literature on the strains of adolescence and youth. Writers like Kenneth Kenniston (1960), David Matza (1964) and Alvin Schoor (1971) have all endeavoured to conceptualise the subjective processes associated with the transition to 'adulthood' in America, and tried to understand the circumstances that may lead to a drift into sporadic or committed delinquency. In 1956, at the height of the Cold War, Paul Goodman had the courage to give voice, in *Growing Up Absurd*, to the fears and anxieties which he believed to be common among all young people: that the pains of growing up could and should be eased by a sense that the adult world might be a worthwhile one, a target worth aiming for both at school and in one's own personal life. At the time, of course, the most widespread concern among young people focused on the arms race and its potential consequences, but there was also an anxiety, which Goodman shared, that the world of employment - especially as driven by the giant corporations of the American economy - demanded from the young an unhealthy level of conformity to authority. Much of the youth trouble of the 1950s was seen as an entirely explicable expression of the rebelliousness of the young against the stultifying demands of the adult work-world of late fifties America.

But at least there *was* a world of work, with considerable security of tenure and comfortable salaries. The world that confronts young people in the 1990s, especially in the less competitive economies of the new global economic order (such as Britain) looks very different indeed. High levels of unemployment have continued throughout the 1980s and 1990s, with heavy concentrations of long-term joblessness in particular areas of our larger cities. Thousands of young people in the last 15 years have faithfully submitted themselves to what one commentator has called the 'magic roundabout' of job-training schemes of one kind or another, only to have their hopes of real work continually smashed and their transition to full financial independence either delayed or indefinitely suspended. Unknown numbers of young people and young adults in the most benighted parts of our cities see the only opportunity for an income, and for access to the continuing enticements of the consumer society, as being the illegitimate economy of property crime and the drugs trade. But even for children and young people in more privileged areas, a world in which political leaders can only conjure up hope by reference to the ever elusive 'green shoots of recovery', and where economists now speak of a prospect 'jobless growth', is a very frightening prospect.

The withdrawal by the Government of different forms of state benefit (including income and housing support) has cut off many thousands of young people from the possibility of any independence from parents. Students in higher education, having also had their entitlements to state support either frozen or withdrawn, are confronting increasing levels of debt. Even the leisure time of young people in the 1990s is beset by the troubles of a world that seems to have gone wrong, as parents of younger children ever more closely shepherd them from school to home, and parents of teenagers worry about the threats of drugs and AIDS, as well as the danger of violence and assault. Problems of homelessness among the young are increasing with great rapidity (the very visible evidence of this being the number of young beggars now encountered on the streets of our cities); and there are widespread reports of a rapid increase in teenage suicides, and of steep escalations in cases of depressions, anorexia and drug abuse among the young.

Or at least these are the fears. There is no more certainty about the condition of youth in the 1990s as there was in the 1950s, and in the aftermath of the appalling murder of toddler James Bulger by two 10 year-old boys many more anxieties have surfaced. In response to this incident, and the general climate of fear surrounding it, we have been treated to a massive dose of rhetoric by our current political leaders, most often on the moral failings of parents. What we have had far too little of - in part because of the preoccupations of the media, politicians and certain criminologists with spectacular stories of delinquency and youthful pathology - are measured and detailed studies of the lives that young people actually lead, and the ways in which the various problems of our time, like drug-related crime, feed into their lives as challenges to be understood and faced. We have one now.

Cautionary Tales is an important and pioneering study in several different senses. Arising out of a survey of 11-15 year-old children conducted in four schools in different areas of Edinburgh in 1990, and a number of taped interviews with small groups of boys and girls from those same schools, the book is best described as a study of 'the place that crime occupies' in the lives of young people. What we hear, loud and clear, are the voices of Scottish children, ranging widely across the question of crime as *they* see it affecting their lives. There is discussion of actual instances of victimisation and harassment, especially - though by no means only - of young girls, as well as accounts of the fear and anxieties of children as a whole and their practical strategies for dealing with such fears. We are also presented with children's perceptions of urban space and territory, and we understand how quickly they have learnt about the reputations of particular urban areas (most evidently in Scotland, of the 'schemes'). The study also provides a clear sense of the way that children manage their relationships with adults and with school, as well as with the police. Most importantly of all perhaps, we obtain a vivid impression of how crime and other problems in the lives of these Scottish children are a problem for all the children studied, regardless of their class background or area of residence. To anyone who has conducted similar research elsewhere in the United Kingdom in recent years the accounts presented here have a very familiar character: they speak to the conditions of children's everyday experience of life in urban Britain in the 1990s well beyond the city limits of Edinburgh.

There is plenty of statistical information in this study, notably in respect of the widespread experience of criminal victimisation among young people. These figures may grab the attention, as they did in press reaction to the earlier release of some of the material in Scotland. But perhaps the central importance of this contribution to the debate about crime in Britain is the way it grounds crime and fear of crime - in a qualitative and quantitative sense - in the mundane experiences of children, whether in their neighbourhood or 'down town'. In this respect, *Cautionary Tales* is in the tradition of the studies of 'everyday fears' developed by feminist criminologists in the 1980s, most notably by Betsy Stanko (1990). What this study shares with that significant tradition is an interest in how different social groups - in this case young people - manage the routine fears of life in urban Britain in the 1990s. There can be few more important issues for our times, for parents, those who work with young people and - not least - for children themselves.

Ian Taylor
Professor of Sociology
University of Salford

April 1994

References

Cohen, S. (1972), *Folk Devils and Moral Panics*, Martin Robertson: Oxford.
Goodman, P. (1956), *Growing Up Absurd*, Vintage Books: New York.
Kenniston, K. (1960), *The Uncommitted: Alienated Youth in American Society*, Harcourt Bruce Jovanovitch: New York.
Matza, D. (1964), *Delinquency and Drift*, Wiley: New York.
Schorr, A. (1975), *Children and Decent People*, Allen and Unwin: London.
Stanko, E. (1990), *Everyday Violence: How Men and Women Experience Sexual and Physical Danger*, Pandora: London.

Preface

The substance of this book first appeared in 1990 as a report to Lothian Regional Council, at a time when the questions that interested us were of somewhat marginal concern to criminologists and policy-makers alike. Since then many of the issues raised by *Cautionary Tales* have come to assume a more prominent place on the criminological research agenda. The last few years have witnessed, for the first time, the inclusion of 11 to 15 year-olds in the national victimisation surveys carried out by both the Home Office and The Scottish Office. There has also been an increasing amount of research attention devoted to questions of young people's safety and victimisation, and to young people's experiences of the criminal justice system as victims and witnesses (Morgan and Zedner, 1992).

We have during this period continued, in different ways, to be involved with these issues: Simon Anderson through his work on the Scottish Crime Survey, Richard Kinsey by extending the present research into rural and small town schools in Lothian region, Ian Loader in his doctoral research on young people and police accountability, and Connie Smith through her work at the Royal Scottish Society for Prevention of Cruelty to Children.

The chief consequence of this is that our ideas have developed in ways that are not altogether reflected in the account that follows. For example, recent work on the fear of crime (Kinsey and Anderson, 1992; Sparks, 1992) has complicated the issue in ways that our discussion of 'fear' among young people does not entirely anticipate. We further believe that the use of the term 'strategy' to describe the ways in which young people manage risk in public places over-rationalises the processes that occur and is in significant respects inadequate. The discussion of young people and the police is also insufficiently alive to the generic limitations of policing vis-a-vis young people's safety, though we are still of the view that young people's victimisation is not taken anywhere near seriously enough by the police (Loader, 1993).

Subsequent developments - and the continuing public fixation with questions of 'juvenile crime' - have, however, served merely to accentuate the relevance of the original study. We have therefore decided to publish the report - which was originally circulated only among a few criminological colleagues and interested practitioners - in a more permanent and widely available form. In so doing, we have not made any substantial revisions to the text and have limited ourselves to slight editorial corrections and stylistic revisions.

Simon Anderson   Central Research Unit, The Scottish Office
Richard Kinsey   School of Human Studies, University of Teeside
Ian Loader   Department of Criminology, Keele University
Connie Smith   Royal Scottish Society for Prevention of Cruelty to Children

April 1994

Introduction

It may well be that some of the young people we have interviewed and spoken to during the course of this research will end up with multiple convictions, and even in prison. We can, however, be sure that this will be true of only a very small minority, albeit mainly male and working class. It is also true, however, that the majority of the young people we interviewed had committed and witnessed offences, had been victims of crime, and had experienced adversary contact with the police. While it is essential that we understand the process through which certain people are differentially selected, labelled and processed through the criminal justice system (thereby maintaining Scotland's record of imprisoning more people *per capita* than almost any other country in western Europe) this is not the object of the present study. Rather, we are concerned with the place that crime, in its different dimensions, and the criminal justice system - particularly the police - hold in the lives of the vast majority of young people in Edinburgh who do not become 'delinquents'.

In 1989, with funding from Lothian Regional Council, we were able to carry out a small study in Craigmillar, a council estate on the periphery of the city. The research was carried out at a local school, where we interviewed 250 young people aged between 11 and 15. In terms of the methods employed, the research proved very successful but the findings were surprising and in some cases alarming. First of all, we discovered a high level of criminal victimisation, much higher than that experienced by the local adult population, as was subsequently shown by the Edinburgh Crime Survey (Anderson *et al.*, 1990). For example, within the previous nine months, two-thirds of the girls interviewed had been harassed by adults following them on foot or by car, asking them things, shouting or calling after them or threatening them. The situation appeared no less difficult for boys, some 39% of whom had been victims of assault and 33% of threatening behaviour in public places.

Secondly, we discovered that not only were young people very often the victims of crime, they also witnessed a considerable amount of crime: no less than a third of those we interviewed had seen a car being broken into, 23% had witnessed a local housebreaking, and 66% had seen someone assaulted and injured. In short, contact with crime was a routine experience.

The fears and anxieties occasioned by such incidents appeared further compounded by a very high level of adversary contact between young people and the police. No less than 62% of boys told us they had been moved on or told off by the police, while 39% had been stopped and questioned and 22% had been arrested and detained at the local police station. Thus, from their point of view, it often seemed that the police were there to make trouble for young people rather than to solve it.

Yet despite this, the young people interviewed were by no means aggressively anti-police. Rather, they displayed a deep ambivalence, born out of the contradiction between their needs as victims of crime and their experience of the police as adversaries. As one young girl we interviewed put it: 'They're always moving us on for something, but they never do anything about all the perverts and the weirdoes.'

Finally, we found that offending was widespread - our figures showed that 9% of boys had broken into houses, 12% had been involved in car theft and 15% had broken into cars, while a majority of the young people interviewed had committed acts of vandalism or other petty offences. Obviously, this too complicated their relations with the police.

These results were clearly important and raised a number of difficult questions. Why was there such an enormous discrepancy between our findings and official estimates of both the victimisation of young people and of their involvement in offending? Were such problems specific to this particular estate or would the same patterns be found in other areas of the city - in middle class residential areas of the city or in the suburbs, for example? What, if any, was the relationship between offending, witnessing and being the victim of crime?

Without knowing the answers to such questions, we were reluctant to publish our findings, as we feared that the press would seize on the more sensational aspects of the research. By doing so, we felt, we might indirectly reinforce existing stereotypes and contribute to the problems, instead of helping to resolve them. Indeed, our fears that the findings would have been misreported were partly confirmed by a series of irresponsible reports in the *Edinburgh Evening News*, which chose to sensationalise the very fact that the follow up research was being conducted, at the cost of considerable anxiety for parents and both time and money in terms of completing the research.

In order to address the questions raised by the original study, the Regional Council awarded us a small grant of £7,500 to extend the survey to four additional schools in other parts of the city. Headteachers and staff at in four schools in different areas of the city agreed to us interviewing their pupils. Questionnaires were completed by 892 pupils at the schools in March and April 1990. These were followed up in face to face interviews and informal discussion sessions with a total of 120 pupils (30 from each school).

At this point, we should make it very clear that this is not a study of the schools themselves or in any way related to the quality of educational provision. Nor is it about the home or the family. Rather, the object of this research is to gain a better understanding of the public rather than private lives of young people. Thus we focus on events, incidents and time spent in the streets and other public places rather than upon incidents occurring in the home or in school.

We chose to emphasise this particular aspect of young people's lives for two reasons. First, the results of the pilot study in Craigmillar had suggested that general understanding of young people's experience of crime outside the home was severely limited. Secondly, we felt that basic research into the public aspects of young people's lives was a necessary and fundamental counterpart to the extensive research and policy development presently being undertaken in areas, such as child sexual and physical abuse, children's rights and the provision of welfare and legal services for the young.

In effect, therefore, the four schools at which the fieldwork took place schools did no more than provide us with a sample of young people drawn from different parts of the city. In no sense, therefore, should this work be used as a standard against which to judge or criticise the schools themselves or the staff, who were of enormous help to us and to whom we are very grateful.

This is not to say, however, that in a wider and perhaps more abstract sense 'school' is unimportant to this study. Obviously, for young people school is a significant and central aspect of their lives. But for this research it has a particular significance: school is like a magnet which literally draws young people together and very firmly dictates their use of the city, public places and facilities. Thus, although the Parents' Charter may have altered the social composition of some schools and widened the catchment areas of others, the school a young person attends significantly influences the cultural identity and social lives of pupils in the world outside.

The four schools were selected on two simple grounds: first, they were very different from one another in terms of the areas and communities in which they were situated; and secondly, for comparison with the adult population, we wanted to select schools in areas covered by the Edinburgh Crime Survey we carried out on behalf of the Safer Edinburgh Project in the second half of 1989 (Anderson et al., 1990). The schools, or rather the areas they serve, are described in detail in Chapter 1.

As mentioned earlier, the fieldwork for the research was carried out in the spring of 1989 and had two main elements. First, a self-completion

3

questionnaire was given to a total of 427 girls and 465 boys between the ages of 11 and 15. Including the Craigmillar study, this provided a total sample of 1142. The questions covered a wide range of subjects, but were broadly aimed at building up a picture of young people's social lives and expectations, within which to analyse their contact with different aspects of crime (as victims, witnesses or offenders) and their contact with the police (both as recipients of police services and in terms of 'adversary contact', that is police action taken against them).

The questionnaire was administered to groups of 15-20 pupils by members of a full-time research team based in the Centre for Criminology and the Social and Philosophical Study of Law at the University of Edinburgh. Undertaken during school hours, it took on average about thirty five minutes to complete. Teachers were not present during this time and the anonymity of the survey was thoroughly emphasised. To gain a representative sample while ensuring the minimum interruption of the curriculum and inconvenience to the schools, the questionnaires were administered to non-streamed, mixed ability Social Education classes.

After preliminary analysis of the questionnaires, follow-up interviews were conducted in small, single sex groups of five boys and five girls from each year (S1 to S3). This particular procedure was adopted following the original pilot, when we had experimented with individual interviews - these were found too intimidating, especially by the younger pupils - as well as with mixed groups - these we found unproductive as the boys tended to dominate and exclude the girls.

The interviews, which were tape-recorded, were unstructured and lasted between thirty and sixty minutes. The idea was to let the children tell us about their own experiences and feelings about crime and policing, with as little direct intervention from the interviewer as possible. Generally speaking, this worked extremely well and, with only occasional prompts, the young people appeared to talk quite freely amongst themselves about the issues raised in the questionnaire. Quotations from these interviews have been used throughout the text to give added depth to the quantitative findings.

Surveying young victims

The basis of this research lies in the application of techniques now widely used for estimating the level of criminal victimisation among the adult population (Sparks *et al.*, 1977). To our knowledge, however, this is the first time this method has been used in a large scale study of young people and crime. In this section, therefore, we shall briefly describe the basic methodology employed and some of the difficulties encountered.

Originally, the application of sample survey techniques to the measurement of crime was a reaction against an over-reliance on official

4

criminal statistics. The unreliability of police statistics as a measure of the extent of crime is now generally accepted, most obviously because they only include crimes and offences notified to the police and thus cannot include the *majority* of offences which are not reported. Also, they will frequently say nothing about 'offensive incidents' which fall outside the formal categories of the criminal law, such as sexual or racial harassment.

To counter these problems crime surveys have been used, both locally and nationally, in which a sample of the population is asked directly whether they have been victims of certain types of personal and household crime over a fixed period of time (usually a year) and if so whether the offence was reported to the police. Provided the sample is properly representative, the findings can be then used to estimate the rate of actual victimisation throughout the whole population and the so-called 'dark figure' of crime (that is the amount of crime unreported to the police) can be reliably established. Such studies thus enable policy makers to evaluate the unmet needs of different sections of the population and of particular communities.

The first major crime surveys of this type in Britain were undertaken by the Home and Scottish Offices in early 1981 (Hough and Mayhew, 1983; Chambers and Tombs, 1984) and have been repeated several times since then in order to chart changes in the rate of crime over time. Useful though such work has been in establishing national rates and trends, for the purposes of local policy making they are still no more than a blunt instrument. Thus the results tend to average out the incidence of victimisation across the country as a whole, leading to rather unhelpful observations such as 'the statistically average person' can expect a robbery once every five centuries, the family car to be stolen once every sixty years and a burglary in the home once every forty years (Hough and Mayhew, 1985:15).

Inevitably, therefore, national crime surveys obscure the way in which victimisation is concentrated in different communities and among particular groups within those communities. To remedy these problems, a 'second generation' of local crime surveys have been carried out, usually under local authority funding (Kinsey, 1985; Anderson *et al.*, 1990; Crawford *et al.*, 1990). By drawing samples from small neighbourhoods, these surveys have described much more accurately the experiences of different sections of the population within those areas, highlighting the difference between the 'statistically average person' residing somewhere in a homogeneous Britain and, for example, a 20 year-old black man living in Liverpool 8. This work has been used to evaluate policing strategies, local needs and resource allocation.

But while local crime surveys have successfully illustrated the geographic and demographic location of crime within their sample populations, those populations have been, without exception, *adult* ones - all have been made up of respondents aged 16 or over. This is a serious omission, as it neglects perhaps the most vulnerable group in society - namely children and young people. The notion of the child as a victim is an increasingly familiar one. Yet while a great deal of attention has, rightly, been focused on the issues of child sexual and physical abuse in the home, there has been little or no attempt to document patterns of other forms of victimisation among young people in Britain; this, despite the fact that official statistics on victimisation and offending among young people are even less reliable than those for the adult population.

This research is intended to help fill that gap. Deliberately, therefore, we avoided questions of physical and sexual abuse in the home or in school - partly because valuable work on the subject was going on elsewhere and partly because we did not feel that a self-report questionnaire or interviews in a school-room setting were appropriate ways of investigating such issues. Our focus then was specifically on things that happen to children when they are out in the streets or in other public places.

But while this was primarily a victim survey, and was concerned with young people as recipients of police services, we felt it was also important to understand the other ways in which they come into contact with crime and the law. We therefore included a series of questions about incidents they had witnessed taking place, offences they had committed themselves, and direct contact they had with the police. By doing so, we hoped to overturn the usual emphasis on the 'delinquent' - the young person as perpetrator rather than as victim of crime - and show the way in which the different points of contact with crime are interconnected.

This research, then, reflects many of the methods and themes of the local crime surveys. Its focus, however, is somewhat different from those that have gone before. In the following section we will examine some of the problems of using this type of survey technique, before moving onto a more detailed discussion of our reasons for concentrating on the victimisation of young people.

Problems with self-reporting techniques

The principal method employed by this and similar studies is the self-report questionnaire. This is, of course, not a completely trouble-free way of collecting data and a number of questions arise. At a general level it must be asked whether or not the technique actually works? Does it give us a more accurate picture of levels of victimisation and offending than the official crime statistics? More specifically, are there particular problems with using this technique to study young people?

Two general points can be made about the efficacy of such methods. First, in a victim survey, it is only possible to ask people about crimes that they know have happened to them. This means that while it is possible to arrive at reasonable estimates of the level of most types of personal and

6

household crime, we can say nothing about victimisation arising out of corporate crime or so-called 'victimless' crime.

Secondly, people can only be asked about their experience of victimisation or offending using concepts that are meaningful to them. This is a general problem with such research, but is particularly true of work with children, who tend to perceive the world in ways far removed from the closely defined legal categories of the criminal justice system. The findings of self-report surveys are, therefore, not always easy to compare directly with police statistics. For example, in this survey and in the Edinburgh Crime Survey (Anderson *et al.*, 1990) we asked respondents if they had been 'worried or frightened' by people following them, staring at them or asking them things. While it is quite clear that there are considerable numbers of 'victims' of such behaviour, no such category as 'harassment' exists in law. Indeed, within the conventional assumptions of the criminal law which requires *mens rea* or guilty intent on the part of the perpetrator, the legal definition of such an offence could be difficult and inevitably controversial. This does not, however, diminish the impact of such incidents upon the victim.

Although crime surveys attempt to use categories that are meaningful to the respondent, there may still be problems of comprehension. Again this is a particular problem when undertaking research with young people as there may be literacy or language problems. This is of particular salience to the present study as, for some of the younger children and those with learning difficulties, the questionnaire undoubtedly proved to be too long and too complicated in parts. However, because we administered the survey ourselves, we were able to monitor the progress of the children and identify and assist those having difficulty answering. As the pattern of answers to the vast majority of the questionnaires was logically consistent we are satisfied that lack of comprehension was not a significant problem.

A further difficulty with research of this nature involves the accuracy of recall. Obviously, respondents may simply fail to remember everything that has happened to them. They might forget an incident because they perceive it as trivial or because it had no lasting impact on them. Alternatively, it might have had such a traumatic effect that, consciously or unconsciously, it is suppressed.

A second possibility is that even where the respondent does remember an incident they recall or recount the details of it inaccurately. This is particularly true in relation to the timing of an event. Sparks *et al.* (1977:35) identify the problem of 'telescoping', which happens 'when a respondent remembers and reports an event, but recalls the event as having happened either earlier or (more usually) later than it in fact did'. Studies of this problem have suggested that there is a slight tendency for respondents to 'telescope' forwards; that is, to project an incident from the past into the reference period of the survey. To counter this, use is often made of a 'bounded' reference period, that is, a time period with particularly salient features. Thus, instead of asking children about things that had happened to them during the last year, we asked them about those things that had happened 'since the start of the last summer holidays', a very clear landmark in their calendar. Despite this, we suspect there was a tendency for children to 'telescope' forwards and report incidents - particularly serious ones - that happened longer ago. However, as there is no adequate means of checking, this is only a suspicion.

A further assumption is that the respondent is not only able to answer accurately, but is also *willing* to do so. In other words we have to confront the difficult question of whether or not respondents were telling the truth. For example, did they under-report by deliberately failing to tell the researchers about incidents in which they had been either victims or offenders? Alternatively, did they report spurious incidents as serious ones, or worse still, did they invent them?

This is a particularly sensitive issue in the context of the present study, as there is considerable debate over whether or not children can be considered reliable subjects for this kind of research and, for that reason, whether the results obtained should be taken into account for purposes of policy development (Box, 1981:ch.3). For such reasons extreme care was taken in the administration of the questionnaire. Thus, there were some pupils, though very few (11), who self-evidently did not take the questionnaire seriously. These were weeded out at the time of completion. Secondly, elements of the questionnaire enabled internal cross-checks for consistency of response and response set. In about a dozen questionnaires, anomalies and 'extreme cases' did appear. However, after very careful consideration of all the individual cases, we decided not to exclude them. We felt it was inappropriate for us to judge their plausibility, indeed to do so would have been to undermine the very basis of the research which was to *listen to* young people rather than impose adult preconceptions upon them.

Finally, through the interviews, we were able to follow up the findings from the questionnaire to see whether, in terms of our own impressions, the results accorded with the way in which young people talked about crime and their experience of victimisation. While clearly this is a question of the professional rather than 'scientific' competence of the researchers, subjectively we were all convinced of the value and the reliability of their comments. For example, some of the more serious findings relate to sexual importuning. On many occasions, young girls related accounts of incidents which were so precise in their description of very small details (like the colour of the scarf she was wearing or the number of the bus she had been travelling on) that credibility was never in doubt.

Perhaps the most convincing demonstration of the reliability of the findings, however, is the extraordinary consistency of the results across the different schools. Very simply, if the young people who took part in the research either deliberately or unwittingly gave false answers, they did so with a consistency and regularity that denies any common sense or, indeed, philosophical conception of the nature of falsehood.

Overall, then, we are confident of the accuracy and reliability of our findings and that they provide a serious index of the kinds of problems the young people routinely face throughout the city. We recognise that there are a number of unanswerables - such as how many of the children misunderstood the questionnaire, made things up or reported incidents from outside the survey's period of reference - but these are part and parcel of any self-report survey and, despite them, we believe the results shed light on an area of victimisation and offending that is remarkably ill-served by the official statistics.

The structure of the book and some theoretical issues

It might be thought from the chapter headings that this study deals with a series of discrete issues. In Chapter 1, we look at the broad social and historical context of crime and the policing of young people in Edinburgh, outlining something of the city's social and spatial divisions as well as questioning some very basic assumptions about the idea of childhood and its implications for understanding victimisation. In Chapter 2, we examine in detail the nature and extent of crimes committed against young people, by adults as well as by others of their own age. Following that, in Chapter 3, we look at other ways in which crime and the fear of crime has an impact upon young people, as witnesses of crime for example, and at the informal strategies and techniques they adopt to cope with crime. In Chapter 4 we explore the nature of their contact with crime as offenders and at some of the popular and populist explanations of 'delinquency'. Finally, we complete the substantive analysis with an examination of young people's relations with the police and their expectations of them.

We want to stress, however, that none of these issues can be understood in isolation from each or any of the others. This is not a study of 'juvenile delinquency'. Our primary focus has been on children as victims of crime and recipients of police services. In part this approach was dictated by what we took to be the exclusive, narrow concern with juvenile delinquency which has dominated both academic and policy discussions of youth and crime. As the results of this study show, the routine and very extensive victimisation of young people in public places has in consequence been hidden from view, if not totally ignored by public services and by adults in general.

However, an exclusive concern with victimisation would similarly distort the place and reality of crime in the lives of young people. At the simplest level, many young people are not only victims of crime, they very often commit the same crimes themselves. Moreover, they witness more crime than adults (much of it serious crime) and they come into contact with the police far more frequently. It would be an exaggeration to say that a young person might be a victim today, an offender tomorrow, a witness the day after, and in trouble with the police the day after that. But, as we shall see, over a period of nine months, a surprisingly high proportion of young people had experienced each and all of these different aspects of crime and policing. Importantly, we shall also see that such experiences mutually interact, often in a contradictory and confusing manner.

One of the most difficult tasks of this project will be to unravel this complex web of interconnections. In attempting to do so, we have employed a very simple theoretical model, which can be represented diagramatically as follows.

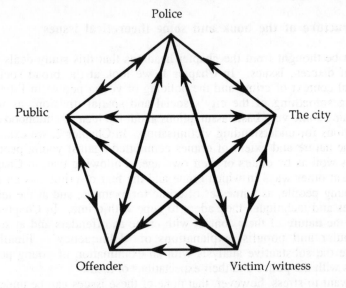

The diagram is intended to show how each element in the process - each point on the pentagon - is defined and re-defined in a continuing social process or dialectic. For example, if we wish to understand the meaning of a particular incident, such as an assault, it is necessary to examine the totality of complex relations which compose it. First, we might begin by looking at the relationship between the victim and the offender in terms of their age, gender or race. Predictably, responses from both the public and the police will vary, for example if the victim is a child and the offender an adult, or if both victim and offender were young teenage males. Immediately, therefore, we have entered the public realm of ideological and moral definition.

Alternatively, the relationship between the victim and offender may be such as to prevent it coming into the public realm, as for example in child abuse or domestic violence. Again, however, an analysis of such incidents

10

which ignored the wider issues of the family or gender would be inadequate. On the other hand, it may be that the victims relations with or perception of the police come into play - he or she may have previously broken the law, or fear discrimination or unfair treatment because of race or age. Then again, the offence may be reported independently by a third party witness, who feels aggrieved despite the views of the victim. Indeed, it is arguable that, in such circumstances, witnesses can themselves be victims and have specific rights as well as duties in relation to the police.

Already the issues are becoming tangled. But we can take it much further. To what extent are public attitudes towards crime shaped or influenced by the police or the courts? For example, how far is present concern in Edinburgh about violent crime in Lothian Road a product of the current police and media campaigns, rather than a reflection of the public's experience of a real problem? How much is it a residue of the city's history? Robert Louis Stevenson, for example, describes Lothian Road in the nineteenth century in terms which, no doubt, the present Chief Constable would endorse.

The location of criminal incidents in different parts of the city may be significant in a number of other ways. Certain crimes are common in certain places by reason of the structure of the urban environment. For example, assaults are, in fact, common on Lothian Road because of the unusual concentration of entertainment facilities in the centre of Edinburgh. This part of the city is thus policed in a manner which in outlying suburban areas would be viewed as inappropriate.

For good and bad reasons, certain places and neighbourhoods in the city have attained reputations as violent or dangerous. These reputations may or may not be merited. Nonetheless, an assault in such an area may take on particular symbolic importance, resulting perhaps in extended coverage in local newspapers and in 'exemplary' judicial sentencing. This in turn may heighten public awareness and fear of crime, producing a greater readiness on the part of the public to report such incidents, and so to an apparent escalation of the problem. Paradoxically, this process of 'amplification' may even increase the likelihood of victimisation. As members of the public adapt their behaviour to avoid certain places, so the empty streets become dangerous and the real risks of crime so much the greater.

Even from this very short account, the complex set of relations running through any analysis of crime should be clear. In the context of the present research, we intend to employ the above model to highlight certain specific and common problems. For example, we will use it both to describe the relationship between offending, victimisation and policing, and to examine the unstated assumptions of policing and their consequences. A specific instance might illustrate this.

As we shall see, over the period of nine months covered by the survey, a very substantial majority of all young people - about two-thirds - had committed minor offences and incivilities, such as petty vandalism and rowdiness in the street. This undoubtedly causes real problems for local residents, and is the subject of continued complaints to the police. During the same period, however, as we shall also see, a very substantial minority of girls - about a third - were victims of serious sexual importuning by men. These incidents were rarely, if ever, brought to the attention of the police. Thus, as far as the police are concerned, young people are brought to their attention as a cause of complaint - that is, as *delinquents,* rather than *complainants.*

Not surprisingly perhaps, this can be the cause of resentment among the young people concerned. They find themselves being moved on and told off by the police for what they see to be trivial and infrequent acts, while the serious offences committed against them receive no attention. The result is classic double-bind. The less they actually report, the less the police can and will do. The less the police do, the greater the resentment. The greater the resentment, the less still is reported. But what is even more significant, the less service young people feel they receive from the police, the more they seek to remedy the situation for themselves. Often this takes the form of young people banding together in 'gangs', which in turn are seen as threatening or provocative by others, so reinforcing perceptions of youth as 'disruptive' or 'delinquent'. The vicious circle tightens.

To attempt to understand relations between young people and the police, *solely* by reference to offending, *or* victimisation, *or* policing, would be to miss the most important point - namely, the symbiotic relationship between the three. Furthermore, to do so would be to reinforce a common and unfortunate tendency. Very often we find the police blamed for deteriorating relations with young people, or conversely, young people indiscriminately labelled as hooligans, thugs and delinquents. Neither interpretation is legitimate. The problems of youth, crime and policing are historically and socially constructed. For this reason our first chapter begins with that history.

12

1 Young people and the city

Introduction

Popular perceptions of different areas of the city change over time, as do the realities of life for residents and their experiences of crime and related problems. In general terms, therefore, we would argue that there can be no understanding of crime without history and no understanding of crime in Edinburgh which disregards the history of the city. At the same time, however, an understanding of young people and crime would be equally impoverished if it failed to recognise the history of childhood and the unique place which children occupy both in the public imagination and in the institutions designed to protect them.

In this chapter, we begin by looking at some of the stereotypes young people themselves have about the city they live in and the areas we have selected for study. This is followed by a brief description of those areas and their history. We do this not only to provide some sense of the differences between those areas for people who are unfamiliar with them, but to emphasise that such reputations have real outcomes for those living there.

Different styles of policing are an obvious case in point. But even more important, perhaps, is the way in which images of the city have tacitly invaded thinking about crime to the exclusion of factors of equal importance. For this reason we include in this chapter a brief review of the 'underclass thesis' - the proposition that problems of youth and crime are geographically focused in certain areas of the city, particularly the 'inner city' and the 'problem estate' where, some have argued, completely different sets of values have developed, particularly in relation to work, school and the family (Murray, 1984, 1990; Wilson, 1987; Baker, 1990). This argument is challenged by the results of the present research, where remarkably little difference is found between areas in terms of young people's values and concerns. Indeed, at many points in this study we have found that similarities between young people of different backgrounds far outweigh their differences - victimisation and offending provide but two examples.

There is within both political and popular culture a marked reluctance to take seriously the claims and experiences of young people. In the last section of this chapter, therefore, the concept of 'childhood' is discussed. In particular we look at the modern history of childhood which gave rise to the idea that children should be 'seen and not heard'. Only through this history and its specific place in the history of the city can their actual experiences, described and analysed in the remainder of the report, be understood.

Reputations and the city

Few people would dispute that, within Edinburgh, places like Craigmillar and Wester Hailes have the reputation of being 'problem' areas. On a variety of indicators, they are among the most deprived estates in Scotland. Yet the results of the Edinburgh Crime Survey (Anderson *et al.*, 1990), for example, suggest that the reputations they have acquired locally for crime and delinquency far outstrip reality. In a city like Edinburgh, where poverty has been pushed to the periphery and hidden from the rest of the population, it is particularly easy for such reputations to gain currency. In the absence of first-hand experience of the outlying estates, many young people - and, of course, many adults - base their perceptions of those areas on what they hear of them. In this way, reputations quickly become caricatures and stereotypes, sometimes drawing on familiar media representations of the 'deprived council scheme'; sometimes on the comments of their parents, and sometimes on particular incidents, occasionally experienced directly but more often relayed at second or third-hand:

> SA: *What do you think of Corstorphine? How do you think it compares with other parts of Edinburgh?*
> A: It's probably a more friendly community. Well, there's not as much fighting. You don't see a lot of drug people hanging about the streets like you would in Niddrie or somewhere like that.
> SA: *What are the worst places in Edinburgh to live?*
> B: I'd say Wester Hailes, cos every time you go past there you see quite a lot of the windows are boarded up, there's vandals there maybe, and you hear about things happening in Wester Hailes like say drugs, crime, things like that. Niddrie's got loads of graffiti and smashed windows and all the shops are covered in big metal things.
> *(12 year-old boys, Corstorphine)*

Talking to young people from outside Wester Hailes and Craigmillar, we came across many such examples. Young people interviewed in Corstorphine and central Edinburgh often told us what were clearly exaggerated stories about violence or crime in 'the schemes', though they had only rarely if ever visited them. The following example comes from an interview with 12 year-old boys living in central Edinburgh:

> I ken someone from Niddrie and his back garden's been burnt to the ground. Ken, he's got hedges round his home and he's got big, massive fences to stop people getting in with barbed wire at the top, and they've been bunging matches and that over the fences and all the bushes are all burnt, all black.

Similarly, a group of 15 year-old girls from Corstorphine told us:

A: I went there once *(Wester Hailes)* and nearly got my heid kicked in.
B: Wester Hailes is a dump. You just go in there and there's a pile of kiddies from Wester Hailes and they beat you up. My brother went to Wester Hailes with one of his army pals and a group of casuals beat them up. My brother got a big slit right down his leg and they stabbed him in the front of the heid.

Already at this relatively early age, stereotypes of an *area* are attributed to the personality and characteristics of the *individuals* who live there. Thus, people from Wester Hailes or Niddrie are stigmatised as 'the type of people' who would 'come into your area and break into a house':

SA: Do you think there's much crime in Marchmont?
A: No, not much.
B: If there is crime it's caused by people who don't live in the area, people who come in.
C: It's people who don't live in the surrounding area but maybe they've been in town and they've come past and they've seen the house and thought 'Oh, that's rich pickings'. *(General agreement)*
SA: Where do you think they come from then?
A: Well, places like Niddrie . . .
B: The suburbs.
(14 year-old boys, Marchmont)

> SA: *What sort of person do you think it is that breaks into a*
> *house?*
> A: Hooligans.
> B: Not really hooligans. Hooligans are folk who smash
> windaes, they dinnae really break in.
> C: People that don't get jobs.
> A: People that don't do well at school.
> D: Unemployed, and they look maybe a wee bit scruffy and
> that.
> SA: *Where do you think they'd live?*
> C: In a bad place like Niddrie.
> A: Wester Hailes.
> B: Some parts of Pilton.
> D: But you don't really know that though, where they live,
> cos you dinnae ken them, a criminal . . . Ken, they could
> live in a place like up Regent Street, these huge houses . . .
> Could be a gang of them up my stair.
> *(12 year-old boys, Broughton)*

The social and political process by which areas come to acquire this sort of reputation has been examined extensively in other research (see Baldwin and Bottoms, 1976; Damer, 1989). Such studies have focused particularly upon housing policy and the uneven allocation of resources. Thus, studies by Damer in Govan and by Bottoms and Baldwin in Sheffield have paid particular attention to local authority housing policy and the way in which it contributes to the process of neighbourhood decline. Indeed, within criminology, there is a long tradition of 'ecological' or 'area studies' upon which we shall draw presently.

For the moment, however, we are more concerned with young people, their perception of such processes and the effect that reputations and labels have upon their everyday lives. Among young people in Wester Hailes we found not only awareness of this process, but also an acute resentment of it:

> A: People from, like, in the middle of town, if you mention
> Wester Hailes they've probably never been in it, they just
> think of AIDS and drugs and that.
> B: They're just going on what they've heard from other
> people who've heard it from other people.
> *(13 year-old boys, Wester Hailes)*

Young people from both Craigmillar and Wester Hailes complained bitterly of discrimination on the part of employers. A 15 year-old boy, about to leave school, told us how he used his grandmother's address when applying for jobs as she lived 'up the toon'. Similarly, a group of 15 year-old girls at Wester Hailes all believed that coming from that area would affect their employment prospects:

> A: Cos if you go for a job and that and they say 'Where do you come from?' and you say 'Wester Hailes' they say 'You're no gettin it. You're trouble.'
> B: 'Dinnae want you. Terrible upbringing.'
> C: A bit of crap or something.
> A: Ken, cos people do put you doon when you say you're from Wester Hailes. Like we went away tae camp with the school and they were saying that we were all trouble-makers and everything. The people at the camp, they said 'Where do you come from.' 'Wester Hailes.' And they said 'Oh no, not Wester Hailes.' As if we were there to cause trouble.
> CS: *Why do you think that is?*
> B: Because of the reputation it's got.
> A: People have given it a reputation.
> B: Then people get in trouble and the place jist gets a worser name and the place get messier with writing and spray painting.

Paradoxically, the labelling of 'bad areas' can have unintended consequences for the good areas. Thus, one girl from Corstorphine resented the way in which she felt the needs of young people in 'her area' were ignored by the 'big people' in the Council, because Corstorphine was not seen as a 'problem area':

> The people round here got a petition and sent it off to the big people somewhere and said why can't areas round here get more facilities for younger folk. And they said there's not enough vandalism. Like if there was more vandalism they'd get more facilities, like in Wester Hailes and that. They've got the big pool and drama clubs and badminton courts and that. So what they're trying to say, is if we do more vandalism, spray paint and that, we'll get more swimming pools and clubs and that. It's pretty stupid.
> *(15 year-old girl, Corstorphine)*

We were subsequently able to corroborate her story - though the Councillor told it slightly differently. True or not, however, such stories have much to reveal. First, they show how, in terms of popular myth, crime is individualised and reduced to a quality of a certain 'type of person' living in certain 'problem areas'. Secondly, for many of the young people we spoke to, there was clear resentment of the way in which if you were

17

young and came from certain areas you were seen as trouble by the 'big people'. We shall look at the 'problem of youth' presently. First, we need to examine the way in which area reputations have developed and their implications for the findings of this study.

Social area and social class

For purposes of comparison with the findings from the pilot study, we selected four schools in very different and distinct areas of the city. Craigmillar and Niddrie, as we have seen from the comments of young people living elsewhere, clearly enjoy a particular place in the city's demonology. Indeed, its current reputation is one which long pre-dates the building of the scheme in the late 1920s to house residents from the original 'inner city', the slum areas of the Old Town.

Although there has been subsequent development of the scheme in the post-war period, with the construction of high-rise flats in the Greendykes area in the 1960s, and low-rise sheltered housing after that, Craigmillar retains the characteristics of a relatively settled, but persistently deprived area. Thus in 1936, the Edinburgh Council of Social Services reported that 'health facilities were totally inadequate; shops were too few, and expensive, and carried a limited range of goods; and that there was a dampness problem in the houses' (Hague, 1984:182). Male unemployment stood at 40% and cuts resulted in severe overcrowding at primary school level. By the 1980s, if anything, the situation was even worse, and Craigmillar was described as one of the most deprived housing schemes in Scotland (Garner, 1989) - 51% of the children interviewed in the pilot study had neither parent in full-time employment, while in 1985, almost six in ten of the pupils at the school qualified for free school meals (Lothian Regional Council, 1988a).

According to the headteacher at the local school, 'the main characteristic of the community is isolation - geographic isolation - which leads to isolation in terms of poverty.' In many respects, therefore, Craigmillar conforms with the image of the Scottish peripheral housing scheme: depressed, dismal and hidden from view. For many Craigmillar people, there is very little contact with the rest of the city. Car ownership is low (25% of households, compared with an average of 50% across the city as a whole - Anderson *et al.*, 1990) and many residents rarely visit the city centre (Lothian Regional Council, 1988b). In terms of policing, it is regarded as one of the 'busiest' areas of the city. Crime is said to be higher than elsewhere and policing highly visible.

In contrast to Craigmillar, therefore, we selected Corstorphine. On the other side of the city but about the same distance from the centre as Craigmillar, the differences could not be more stark. The 'village' of Corstorphine is predominantly a middle class commuter suburb, although it

18

includes a large stock of council-built housing. Unlike Craigmillar and Niddrie, where the boarded-up windows and void flats are commonplace, the council housing in Corstorphine is, as it has always been, among the most sought after in the city. There one notices the grass, the trees, the view across the Firth, and the number of newly privatised front doors. Indeed, as of June 1990, 1264 council houses in Corstorphine and Clermiston had been bought by their tenants, in contrast to just 34 in the Craigmillar area.

In the main, however, Corstorphine is a model of modern suburbia, with very recent, as well as immediately post-war, private developments, much as one will find in any provincial British city. The process of suburbanisation began much earlier, of course, with the advent of the local railway system in the nineteenth century. Still earlier, there was the village of Corstorphine - a folk memory of which still lingers among its new middle class professionals and managers. In terms of our sample, however, the children of the wealthier 'professional classes' may be under-represented, as large numbers attend private schools in Edinburgh. As the headteacher at the local school put it:

> If you were looking at the occupation of the parents of the children at this school you would see a lot of people in banking, a lot in insurance and a lot of people who are upwardly mobile - but not your professional classes, as in Edinburgh many of them will be going into schools in the private sector.

Also on the west of the city and at a similar distance from the centre, is Wester Hailes. About two miles from Corstorphine, Wester Hailes is a place that few of the middle classes will visit. A green belt development in the late 1960s, it covers 287 acres, trapped between arterial roads in and out of the city and dissected by the canal, a railway line and overhead pylons. The sloping site required embankment and steep slopes up to the feeder roads so that an air of artificiality pervades the whole area. The original consultants had recommended that 'the basic idea of urban enclosure should be all pervasive'. In that, if in nothing else, they were proved right.

A mixture of high and low rise housing, Wester Hailes witnessed almost immediate physical deterioration of its housing stock, a rapid turn-over of tenants, and a concentration of social problems associated with demographic instability and deprivation. The first residents arrived in 1968. By 1972 the scheme had already proved 'difficult to let' and the council made a block of eighty five flats available for student accommodation simply to guarantee at least some income. By 1973, the Social Work Department reported that over 86% of the children in the scheme lived in families at or below the poverty level.

The contrast with the immediately adjacent private development at Baberton could not be more immediate: while Baberton has a density of population of 20 per acre, Wester Hailes was planned at 100 per acre. Originally intended for a mobile, working population, each flat was allocated its own parking space - the planners never foresaw the social dislocation that was to accompany unemployment in the eighties. The headteacher described the area in terms unrecognisable alongside the comforts of Corstorphine:

> Just one type of housing, all council housing. At one point there were 18,000 people living in Wester Hailes. That's now declined to around 12,000 to 13,000. There's a mixture of two and three rise blocks and 12 story blocks. Some areas are dominated by the blocks completely, in other areas the blocks just stand like isolated sentinels in the environment. The area was built 15 years ago and designed to allow everyone to have a car. There are parking spaces everywhere in Wester Hailes and hardly a damned car to be seen because of the poverty of the area.

For the outsider, first impressions of Wester Hailes are strangely grim, despite the uniform light grey of the buildings and the open spaces. As one boy from Craigmillar put it, 'I go to Wester Hailes every week to see ma uncle. Even when its sunny it's dark.'

The two other schools we chose are both situated in central residential areas of Edinburgh. They share a common history but a very different present, representing as sharp a spatial division of the central area of the city as residential segregation already described in relation to Corstorphine and Wester Hailes. The first of these serves the more affluent middle classes which cluster together in areas, such as Morningside, to the south and south west of the city.

Though close to the centre of town, the school is situated in the heart of Marchmont, a residential area of private, high quality, tenement housing built in the second half of the nineteenth century. The streets are wide and quiet, gardens are neatly kept and the Meadows (the site of the old Burgh Loch, which was drained as part of the eighteenth century improvements) are in immediate reach. Today, the area is overwhelmingly middle class in character and, close to the university, is favoured by students and university lecturers, as well as by other professionals.

The school's population is more mixed than this picture of Marchmont might suggest, however. Closer to the centre of the city is Tollcross, an area of late predominantly nineteenth century working class tenement housing at the west end of the Meadows, a later adjunct of the Old Town. Once a thriving commercial area but now in decline, its population is employed mainly in clerical and skilled and unskilled jobs in the service sector. For the most part however, the school's natural catchment area lies further to the south of Marchmont and is composed predominantly of the wealthier and very wealthy areas of middle class Edinburgh, such as Merchiston, Morningside and the Grange.

Together with Marchmont and Bruntsfield, such areas account for approximately half the school intake while the more working class area of Tollcross contributes barely 10%. Most of the remaining places (about a third) are taken up by children commuting from further afield. Indeed, since the introduction of the Parents' Charter, the academic reputation of the school, its extraordinarily good facilities and its location have attracted pupils from as far away as Dunbar, some 30 miles away. However, a detailed analysis of the sample shows that the young people interviewed come almost exclusively from the south and south west side of the city and the vast majority of them from areas which can reasonably described as affluent middle class.

The second of central Edinburgh schools is in Broughton and serves a much more heterogeneous population to the north east of the city centre. While the population served by the school in Marchmont moves sharply up the social scale as one travels out of the town; the one in Broughton - with the advent of the Parents' Charter - now includes areas of multiple deprivation as well as some more established middle class and recently gentrified tenements close to the city centre.

Like the first, the school serves an area most of which was built towards the end of the nineteenth century or in the early decades of this century. Built in the 1920s, on the site of an old marble works, the school itself appears typically institutional, with a bare concrete playground at the front. At the same time, it is far from under-used, providing a centre for a wide range of community activities. Signs on the doors are multi-lingual; notices on the boards advertise adult education classes; the playground doubles up as a car park for adult evening classes.

Sitting in a hollow, on the east side of the New Town but only ten minutes walk from Princes Street, the immediate surroundings of the school are very different from Marchmont. Up the hill, is Broughton Street, a busy commercial street lined with pubs, grocers and small offices and an important route out of town towards Trinity. Round the corner is a rather shabby Georgian terrace, waiting for gentrification. To the west are the New Town homes of the established *haute bourgeoisie* of Edinburgh, but few New Town residents send their children to this school. Most pupils come from the immediate area of Broughton and further to the north and east: Leith Walk, Easter Road, Abbeyhill and Meadowbank. Some come from further away: from Leith itself and the council schemes in Pilton and Drylaw; and some from as far as Portobello.

But, again, detailed analysis of the sample reveals the geographical and residential segregation of the city. Thus very few of the pupils at the school come from the affluent residential areas to the south west which contribute to the intake at the school in Marchmont. This spatial segregation is reinforced by a strong subjective impression of the cultural differences

21

between the two schools. Thus, in the school in Broughton, young people will use Edinburgh dialect - terms like 'pagger', 'choring', 'barrie' - and, importantly, have a far stronger sense of territorial loyalty identity than their socially mobile, 'well spoken' counterparts from the other side of town. (For the sake of brevity, we have used 'Marchmont' and 'Broughton' to refer to the samples drawn from the schools in those two areas. It should be borne in mind, therefore, that in both cases the samples concerned encompassed a far wider area than the use of these shorthand terms indicates.)

'Two towns more ways than one'

The five schools at which the study has been undertaken in different ways represent the culmination of a long history. We believe that history is critical to the way in which 'social problems' have emerged and are still defined in the city and in particular to the way in which reputations have been ascribed and policing policy has developed.

In 1833, William Chambers described Edinburgh as 'two towns more ways than one.' It contains, he said, 'an upper and an under town - the one a sort of thoroughfare for the children of business and fashion, the other a den of retreat for the poor.' The history of the Old and the New Towns of Edinburgh is too well known to require comment here, though the subsequent history of middle class migration in the nineteenth century and the slum clearances of this century are worth brief consideration - especially as they still play such a significant part in the lives of the young people at the different schools from which we drew our sample.

Originally Broughton and the area to the north east of the city centre were earmarked for the extension of the New Town. Plans for 1842 show the area between and either side of Leith Walk and Easter Road, geometrically laid out in the same crescents and circuses, which made James Craig the early legend of modern town planning. None of this was to happen, however. For as Cliff Hague (1984) - upon whose account we rely heavily - has documented, the Age of Enlightenment was broken up by the Age of the Railway as eighteenth century planning gave way to unregulated, nineteenth century capitalism.

Instead, in the latter part of the nineteenth century, the land earmarked for the extension of the New Town was feued for the development of housing for the 'respectable working class'. Thus, the area to the north east of the city saw a period of extraordinarily rapid, unregulated construction, which continued until 1909 when the building of working class tenements in Edinburgh dried up entirely (Hague, 1984:163). Narrow streets of flat-fronted, plain but substantial tenements, were built for rent to the artisans, tradesmen and the vast numbers of administrative and clerical workers in the financial and commercial sector, who had provided the backbone of the city's success. Criss-crossing the area in and around Leith Walk and Easter Road, these flats - typically with two rooms, a tiny cooking area and a water closet - have remained virtually unchanged and (so far) relatively impervious to the eroding gentrification which has broken up many settled working class areas of other cities.

At the same time, the middle classes on the fringes of the New Town, finding themselves socially and physically squeezed by these developments, migrated in vast numbers to the more ornate, turreted tenements and villas of Marchmont and Morningside in the south west of the city, where a parallel expansion was occurring. The move to the suburbs also intensified: between 1891 and 1901, for example, Corstorphine experienced a 22% increase in its population. As the middle classes moved out, so the older Georgian tenements they left behind were subdivided into rack-rented, multi-occupancy flats. In the hands of private landlords these soon degenerated to match the earlier squalor of the Old Town, which had so appalled Chambers.

By 1918 the Trades Council and the local Labour Party estimated the city urgently needed some 10,000 new houses. By 1921, the Medical Health Officer was reporting mortality rates related to housing problems and housing density. But despite intense pressure and 'a flurry of town planning activity' on the part of the City Council, it was not until 1928 that approval for the first improvement scheme (under the 1909 Act) was granted by the Scottish Board of Health - for a four and a half acre site in Fountainbridge (Hague 1984:164).

It is a picture of inner city decline, recognisable in cities throughout Britain. But with one difference - the inner city slums which disfigured the centre of Edinburgh have now been cleared in their entirety and the urban poor hidden away, either in peripheral schemes such as Craigmillar and Wester Hailes or in the more suburban but still invisible estates such as Pilton and Granton. In a sense, therefore, in comparison with other British cities, Edinburgh is inside out. In Liverpool, Manchester or Leeds the inner city is a visible barrier guarding access to the city centre. In Edinburgh, brutal poverty is now discretely hidden from the public gaze and sentimental attachment to the historic city is left undisturbed.

In the nineteenth century, slum clearance to make room for municipal building was common, Chambers Street being but one example. During the 1930s, however, Edinburgh's inner city underwent major slum clearances for the purposes of re-housing the poor. Indeed, the building industry during this period was the city's largest industrial employer providing 10,600 jobs in 1929 and 13,000 in 1939 (Hague, 1984:180). Thus, despite the depression, throughout the 1930s the decayed and overcrowded slum buildings in Broughton, Leith and St. Leonards were torn down. The poor were quarantined in new estates such as Craigmillar, where the planned development for 8,000 had already reached 10,000 by 1936.

23

Hague sums up the implications this intensive redevelopment had for the delicate social relations and working class culture which had previously existed. As we shall see, this is of continuing importance for young people in the city:

> The inter-war boom therefore extended and consolidated status divisions between housing areas. In particular the development of a stock of council houses brought fresh nuances of respectability and stigma within a working class who had previously shared more uniformly poor housing conditions within the private rented sector. Those rehoused from the slums on infill sites were still surrounded by industries and railways and lived at high densities. The more suburban rehousing schemes were usually close to the old tenement districts - Lochend, Prestonfield, Gorgie, Quarry holes, Piershill, Granton and Pilton. The exception was Niddrie in the Craigmillar area, a more truly peripheral location. Thus low status council housing was predominantly in the north and east of the city. [...] (The) western areas became the locations for higher quality estates, at Stenhouse, Saughton Mains, Chesser, Hutchinson, Saughtonhall and Sighthill. The 'aristocracy of labour' who could afford the higher rents and transport costs and who were perceived to be respectable and deserving tenants, moved to these areas. The only significant high status council development east of the centre was the early scheme at Willowbrae and Northfield, close to the amenity of Holyrood Park. (Hague, 1984:182)

Already, the implications of this relocation should be apparent for the selection of our sample. To the west, in Corstorphine, we have the suburbanised middle classes - 'pioneer Edwardian commuters' as Hague calls them - later to be joined by the respectable 'aristocracy of labour'; to the south east, lies the peripheral scheme of Craigmillar while to the north and east, the heterogeneous population served by the school in Broughton. The south and south west, in contrast, lies the area served by the school in Marchmont, untouched by council housing and secure in its newly acquired affluence.

Despite these efforts (however they stand the judgement of time), immediately after the war it was estimated that Edinburgh could had over a quarter of a million residents living in unfit or sanitarily sub-standard housing (Abercrombie and Plumstead, 1949:88). Between 1949 and 1958 almost 9,000 houses were built in the private sector, most of these in suburban areas such as Corstorphine. In the public sector, the 4,000 pre-fabs which had been erected at the end of the war had barely scratched at the surface. By the fifties, central government concern with cost and the local shortage of land became the overriding factors in design and construction of public housing. The first multi-storey block in Edinburgh was built in Gorgie in 1952. By 1961 the council had only a two-year supply of building land available when the census revealed that one house in four had no bath. The solution was sought, in part, in the development of Wester Hailes.

By the 1970s, therefore, it might seem the City Fathers of Edinburgh had finally realised the ambitions of their forebears. In 1835, Lord Cockburn had set the tone, railing against the imminent arrival of 'weavers, calico printers, power looms and steam engines, sugar houses and foundries in Edinburgh!' The city, he said:

> should survive on better grounds, on our advantages as the metropolis, our adaptation for education, our literary fame, and especially on the glories of our external position and features [...] undimmed by the black dirty clouds from manufactures, the absence of which is one of the principle charms of our situation. (Cited in Hague, 1984:137)

Of course, the corruption of industry and the organised working class never really disturbed a city built upon financial rather than industrial capital and where industrial employment was almost exclusively for local consumption. Thus, between 1841 and 1901, clothing was the largest industrial occupation. Together with the manufacture of consumer goods such as leather, glass-ware, furniture, jewellery in the small workshops (still visible round the back of the Cowgate and scattered throughout Leith) local labour serviced the middle classes. Above all, 'there was domestic service, a more significant employer than any industrial group and a further testimony to the importance of the middle class consumer market in the city' (Hague, 1984:137).

Thus, although poverty and class divisions were endemic, there is a sense in which, at the end of the nineteenth century, the city was more integrated than it is today. Certainly there were still the two towns - the New and the Old, the upper-town and the under-town - but people lived in such social and economic proximity that they lived one history. Today, the poor of Wester Hailes and Craigmillar share their history but in geographic isolation, invisible to the majority of residents of the city.

But the history which gave birth to Wester Hailes and Craigmillar also gave birth to the other parts of the city and to the young people who live there. As a result, the school in Broughton, with its heterogeneous population is perhaps the closest Edinburgh has to an 'inner city' school, though it lacks the extreme poverty that characterises such schools in, say, Manchester or Liverpool. The voluntary migration of the middle classes to Marchmont, Morningside, and the Grange and later to Corstorphine is part of the same movement. Thus underlying the experiences of young people

25

and the reputations and views they hold of each other is the political economy of a city, which eventually led to the social divisions which have prompted the description of Edinburgh as 'the most sharply divided (of any) British settlement for which we have appropriate studies' (McCrone and Elliot, 1989:66).

Young people in the city

Hopefully, from this brief history, it can be seen how images of different areas of the city have been constructed historically and have become deeply ingrained in the class structure and culture of the city. Indeed, we saw examples of this in the first section of this chapter. Such reputations will have been handed on through parents and grandparents but are, perhaps, gradually being displaced by the stereotypical images of the tabloids and the television documentary.

The power of such reputations and stereotypes extend far beyond the stories and accounts given by young people, however. Among academics and practitioners, they set up a range of expectations, not only in relation to crime but in relation to young people generally - especially those living in the 'inner cities' and 'problem estates'. In this section, we shall discuss very briefly, one important example of such thought, namely the 'underclass thesis', popularised by American academics such as Charles Murray and recently endorsed by, for example, Kenneth Baker, the former Minister for Education (Murray, 1984, 1990; Baker, 1990).

Briefly, it is argued that among certain sections of the population, usually described as living in 'ghetto' areas of the city, a distinct set of cultural values and expectations can be attributed to an emergent 'underclass' which threatens the integrity of middle class standards and in wider terms, conventional society. Associating such values with high levels of crime and violence, Murray (1990) has claimed that in Britain the underclass is rapidly approaching similar proportions to that which he identifies in the States. Indeed, he has cited the fate of Scottish peripheral estates (and, in particular, Easterhouse in Glasgow) as evidence of this process of decline into depredation and violence.

More specifically, it is argued that traditional values of work, school and family have been undermined by the 'incentives to fail' offered by the welfare state. For example, subsidised, public housing is said to have detached tenants from the discipline of market and property values - they have no 'financial stake' in the property and, for that reason, no self-interest in 'maintaining standards' in the community (i.e. to protect the market value of their own houses). Litter, graffiti, vandalism etc., thus become somebody else's problem as mechanisms of informal social control (based on economic self-interest and owner occupation) break down in generalised apathy and disinterest.

Similar claims are made about the collapse of family values. Thus, the less the 'stake in the community', the fewer incentives there are for parents to keep their children under supervision and control. This is compounded by 'incentives to fail', which make it 'profitable to be poor' and for single parents to rear 'illegitimate' children. These further weaken the cardinal virtues of self-interest, self-reliance and individual responsibility. Likewise, in relation to education, the erosion of discipline in the school has been reinforced by an overall 'levelling down' of expectations consequent upon affirmative action and other 'progressive' policies and practices which, more often than not, have precisely the opposite effect from those intended.

Kenneth Baker (1990), in a speech to the Centre for Policy Studies drew heavily on Murray's work, making the connection with the city explicit. Throughout, he drew a contrast between those successful families who 'flocked to the leafy avenues of suburbia to put down roots and buy their first home' and parents of the inner city, who, according to the one teacher he quoted, 'only want their kids out of sight.' These suburban communities, said Baker, 'stand in stark contrast to some areas within our inner cities, where the traditional family leads a fragile existence. High rates of illegitimacy, single parenthood and truancy have had a devastating effect; unemployment and crime rates are way above the national average.'

To counter what he terms the 'crime culture' of the inner city, young people must relearn the values of the suburban family: that it is 'wrong to lie, wrong to steal, wrong to cheat and wrong to bully. It is right to respect your elders, right to know that you can't have everything instantly, right to take personal responsibility for your own actions and, above all, right to help those less fortunate and those weaker than ourselves.' According to Mr. Baker, in the inner cities such 'supposed suburban bourgeois sentiments . . . are under siege.'

Such ideas surface with regularity in any discussion of crime and young people. Indeed, they cannot but remind the reader of the views expressed by 12 year-old boys cited earlier, which we have suggested are rooted in urban history and the political economy of the city. The idea that young working class people hold different values about the family, school and work and are more disposed to crime than other young people is common on both sides of the political spectrum (although the terminology is different) and ought therefore to be given serious consideration.

These are questions that will be returned to on many occasions in the course of this study. For the moment, therefore, discussion will be limited to the more general claim about the lack of attachment to values of work, school and family. According to the 'underclass thesis', we might expect to find significant class differences between young people in terms of their concerns and worries about their employment prospects, about doing well in school and about their families. As the following graph reveals, however, although there were some differences between areas, there was no uniform pattern to substantiate such claims. Indeed, although the differences are not great, it is noticeable that the pupils at the more middle class school in Marchmont tended to worry marginally *less* on all four measures than those at other schools, while young people from Wester Hailes express marginally *more* concern on three measures.

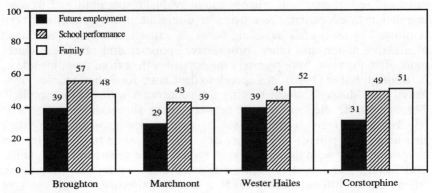

Figure 1.1
Attitudes and values: percentage worrying 'a lot' about work, school and family

Important in this context, however, is not so much the level of anxiety, which is extensive, but the finding that *all* young people tend to worry about much the same things, which suggests that their values are really very similar. Indeed, when we look in closer detail at the results we find minimal differences between young people whose parents are council tenants and those who are owner occupiers; between young people coming from households with no adults in full-time employment and those with one or more in full time work; and, perhaps most significant of all, between those young people who have and those who have not committed offences.

Table 1.1 clearly highlights the overall similarities between the values of young people from different backgrounds and family circumstances. Indeed, it is worth noting that, if anything, the relationships go in the opposite direction to that expected. Thus, for example, larger numbers of young people living in council accommodation, those with neither parent working and those who have committed offences worry 'a lot' about their families and about finding work on leaving school.

Table 1.1
Concerns about school, work and family by tenure, employment status and offending (%)

	Council tenant	Owner occupier	None employed full-time	One or more employed full-time	Offender	Non-offender
School						
Worry a lot	45	45	51	49	50	46
Not much	43	43	36	41	40	43
Not at all	12	12	13	10	11	11
Work						
Worry a lot	40	29	39	33	36	31
Not much	45	56	43	53	51	53
Not at all	15	15	18	14	13	16
Family						
Worry a lot	59	42	57	47	50	44
Not much	29	37	27	37	36	35
Not at all	12	21	15	16	15	21

Note: an 'offender' in the above table includes any young person who has committed at least one of the following offences during the past nine months: rowdiness in the street, fighting in the street, shoplifting, vandalism to property, vandalism to cars, breaking into cars.

These findings suggest that we must be very cautious indeed about commonsense claims which locate problems or problem populations in different areas of the city or among particular sections of young people and 'delinquent subcultures'.

A small problem of credibility

When we set out upon this project, we fully expected to find significant differences between young people in different areas of the city. Indeed, we expected our results would tell a very different story from that which follows. Thus, as in studies of the adult population, we had expected to find clear differences in levels of victimisation, offending and adversary contact with the police among young people living in different areas of the city. Indeed, we expected that social class and area would be the single most important variables in explaining crime and its impact. This was not to prove the case.

When we broadened the survey from Craigmillar into other areas, we found the basic results of the pilot study were repeated across all sections of the population and in all parts of the city. Thus, as will be seen, young people *throughout* Edinburgh had a very high level of contact with crime and the police: the problems we discovered in Craigmillar were not peculiar to that particular area. Rather, it was clear, the findings were peculiar to young people in general.

In sharp contrast to the adult population, therefore, it is essential to recognise that young people of all social classes share *common* experiences of crime in the city, whether as victims, witnesses and offenders, or in terms of their contact with the police. Surprisingly, perhaps, experience of crime among young people appears to cross class and geographical boundaries with relative ease and consistency. This is not to say that, in other respects, questions of social class are irrelevant to the lives of young people. That would be patent nonsense. Rather, our findings suggest that - in some areas of life - their status as 'children' is of greater importance than the socio-economic status of their parents.

Even more striking than the universal experience of crime by young people was their uniformly high contact with crime, much of it serious and most of which adults would find intolerable. Indeed, the contrasts between the lives of young people and those of adults are so stark that a problem of credibility may arise which goes beyond the usual questions of research methodology. In particular, the results suggest that the experiences of most young people are considerably at odds with popular conceptions of childhood as a time of innocence. As adults, we under-estimate and diminish the extent and impact of crime upon young people's everyday lives or even ignore it altogether.

These tendencies are deeply ingrained in many of the institutions concerned with young people's lives, not least the law. Thus, while a philosophy of 'need not deed', and the practice of listening rather than lecturing to young people, informs the Children's Hearings System in Scotland, the evidence of the present research suggests that a very different attitude still shapes many of the routines of the criminal justice system in relation to young people. For example, the notion that children make bad witnesses is reproduced explicitly in legal texts and courtroom practice:

> Children are prone to live in a make-believe world, so that they magnify incidents which happen to them or invent them completely. (Heydon, 1984:84)

In a similar vein, Justice Pickles commented in a *Panorama* television interview that, 'over the years it has been found that children can invent or imagine things that may not have happened at all' (quoted in Spencer and

Flinn, 1990:257). Such attitudes are constituent parts of a 'grown-ups know best' culture in which children are rarely listened to and seldom trusted to tell the truth. As a consequence, young people are often left to deal with problems in their own ways. Though 'grown-ups' may well know *more* about some things, when it comes to the lives children lead away outside the sphere of adult supervision - outside the home, the school room or the youth club - it seems we actually know very little, especially about crime.

'Seen but not heard': the problem of childhood

It should be clear that we take issue with the idea that the evidence of children is dubious or unreliable. In some ways this is implicit in our choice of research method, as there would have been little point in listening to young people had we had no faith in what they had to say. However, the devaluation of the views and opinions of the young cannot be treated simply as an example of judicial idiosyncrasy or senility. Rather it is to be seen as a reflection of a general tendency to treat young people as a separate, powerless and dependent group, who, due to their age and physical immaturity, are deemed incapable of independent rational judgement or action.

Many commentators have pointed out that the special status awarded to children cannot be seen solely in terms of biological or developmental immaturity. Rather, it is a *socially* constructed category and, as such, peculiarly modern. Thus, historians such as Philippe Aries (1962) and J.R. Gillis (1974) have shown that until relatively recently there was a much less rigid distinction between the lives of the young and those of adults. Indeed, in medieval times, according to Aries 'the idea of childhood did not exist'.

To contemporary ears, this sounds radical if not subversive, for the concept of childhood, like that of the family, is now so central to everyday economic and social life that it seems almost sacred. As a result, it is hard to understand the 'Victorian values' which accepted children working in the pits or being sent up factory chimneys. However, what now appears to us morally wrong and 'unnatural', was at that time quite 'normal'.

Aries documents in detail the change from the apparent callousness of seventeenth century parental attitudes, in which children 'did not count' to the child-centred family of the early twentieth century (1962:36-7). When levels of child mortality were so high, the emotional investment we now make in our children was rare, even amongst the aristocracy. In its place was an extended period of infancy (breastfeeding often continued until the age of seven or more), which, if and when successful, was followed by the rapid introduction of the child into the social world of the adult, in which children participated as 'small adults'.

In the eighteenth century, improvements in health and reduction of child mortality rates, especially among the gentry, allowed a new conception of

31

childhood as an 'age of innocence' to emerge. The child was not only to become an object of romantic affection, but also to be protected from the anarchy and corruption of the outside world, a public world which previously had been shared by rich and poor, young and old alike. In the nineteenth century, the move to privatise the family gained extensive ground among the newly affluent middle classes and accelerated rapidly. Aries describes the process in terms which could be directly applied to the history of Edinburgh. Thus in the eighteenth century:

> People lived in a state of contrast; high birth or great wealth rubbed shoulders with poverty, vice with virtue, scandal with devotion. Despite its shrill contrasts, this medley of colours caused no surprise. A man or woman of quality felt no embarrassment at visiting in rich clothes the poor wretches in the prisons, the hospitals or the streets, nearly naked beneath their rags. The juxtaposition of these extremes no more embarrassed the rich then it humiliated the poor [...] But there came a time when the middle class could no longer bear the pressure of the multitude or the contact of the lower class. It seceded: it withdrew from the vast polymorphous society to organise itself separately in a homogeneous environment, among its families, in homes designed for privacy, in new districts kept free from all lower-class contamination. The juxtaposition of inequalities, hitherto seeming perfectly natural became intolerable to it: the revulsion of the rich preceded the shame of the poor. (Aries, 1962:398-9)

Here, then, is the beginning of the modern family and the increasingly rigid separation both of the lives of bourgeois and working class families, and of adults and children within them. Throughout the nineteenth century 'childhood' within the middle class family was progressively extended through the development of formal schooling. Again the child is sealed off from the outside world: in private schools and in privileged isolation from corruption by the lower classes. But, at this point the notion of childish innocence is supplemented by that of the child as partly formed, incomplete and in need of a disciplined, utilitarian introduction to the rigours of the adult world. 'Henceforth,' writes Aries (1962:396), 'it was recognised that the child was not ready for life and that he had to be subjected to a special treatment, a sort of quarantine, before he was allowed to join the adults.'

Thus, through formal education and the underlying notion of 'the formative years', middle class childhood is extended to cover 'adolescence' and restricted to a range of activities which would previously have been unthinkably narrow (Muncie, 1984:81). Around these newly institutionalised boundaries, medical and psychological theory provided expert knowledge of the 'natural' attributes of adolescence (Gillis,

1974:114). In the field of criminology, adolescence - stripped of its history - takes centre stage in the form of the juvenile delinquent. Thus, for the first half of this century at least, research and practice focuses almost to the point of obsession upon juvenile offending and its 'causes' - upon 'maternal deprivation', physical or psychological pathologies, emotional impairment etc. (e.g. Bowlby, 1946).

But more importantly, as industrialisation increasingly demanded a more educated workforce, so childhood was extended to incorporate the working class child. Thus, by the twentieth century, through the system of compulsory state education, the concept, if not the actual experience of 'childhood' was universalised. The lives of *all* children were now to be separated from those of adults, both institutionally and culturally. Certainly, social class remained a determining feature - the experience of a child living in Edinburgh's tenement slums at the beginning of this century was utterly different from that of a child 'schooled' in the ways of the world at a private boarding school. Nonetheless, the importance of the status of 'child' and the universal experiences it brought began to cross other social divisions.

Children and young people - whether rich or poor - share experiences, are victimised and then discounted *because they are children*. The parallel here with the socially constructed status of women in the nineteenth century and contemporary forms of sexism is, we think, self-evident but useful. Just as women were denied status at law - as having no legal capacity and no political rights - so children are still denied credibility and their accounts dismissed as 'childish'.

We are not suggesting, as have some (Holt, 1975:114-205; Farson, 1978:325-8), that children should be accorded exactly the same rights and responsibilities as their elders, nor that they should have the right to determine fully their own lives. Nor are we suggesting that we should return to a conception of children as simply 'small adults' sharing the same cognitions, emotions and perceptions as older people. On the contrary, throughout this research, it was obvious to us that young people conceptualise the world very differently from adults, if for no other reason than that they have experienced less. Michael Freeman pithily summarises the basic point that needs recognition: we must 'provide a childhood for every child and not, as Farson and Holt would, an adulthood for every child' (Freeman, 1983:3).

In recent years, much public and political debate has revolved around notions of childhood and the relationship between children and young people and wider society. Commentators of both Left and Right have been concerned with the impact of economic and social change on young people's lives. For example, the opening up of youth markets in clothes, popular music, etc in the post-war period, has meant that in certain aspects of their lives children once again grow up more quickly. Young people are today offered choices and make demands that, even thirty years ago, were unavailable to them. On this dimension, childhood has contracted. In other respects, however, it has lengthened. In the immediate post-war period boys suddenly became 'men' with compulsory national service. Girls got married earlier and became 'women' with motherhood. The change in status was visible. Today, we quite readily talk of 'young people' until their mid-twenties. Styles of dress, forms of entertainment and many other aspects of social life have become blurred and increasingly difficult to differentiate.

Such renegotiation of the boundaries of childhood has posed certain problems in choosing the categories to employ in this research. Are boys and girls between the ages of 11 and 15 'children', 'adolescents' or are they 'young people'? In terms of the market place they are clearly young people; in other respects, in politics and the more paternalist enclaves of education and the welfare state, they are still children - a separate, powerless and dependant group. In terms of the criminal justice system and its associated disciplines they are 'adolescents'. In this latter world, especially, the problems young people as victims and the demands they have as recipients of the criminal justice system are simply not recognised.

For the purpose of this research, in which we are speaking of 11 to 15 year-olds, we have adopted the term 'young people', although we are far from wholly satisfied with it. It must be recognised that young people in this age group are distinct, if for no other reason that they have still to acquire a working knowledge of the vast array of formal and informal rules which govern everyday life. Indeed, in the course of this report we shall suggest that contact with crime - as victims and witnesses as much as offenders - provides one, very important part of the process of learning those rules. We shall see that young people's *practical* knowledge of these rules is incomplete and that it takes time and experience to gain the most basic working knowledge of them.

Too often, they are left to learn the hard way. As a result, the adult world frequently appears confusing, if not contradictory and duplicitous. For this reason alone, it would be wrong to treat young people as if they were fully assimilated members of society, and to have the same moral and legal expectations of them that one would of an adult. On the other hand, it would be equally wrong to assume that they are unable to grasp, *in principle*, the moral dilemmas of and the problems caused by crime. As we shall see, they are only too aware of the meaning and impact of crime in their own lives - especially as contact with crime and the police is such a common experience. Though their knowledge of the rules is incomplete, their experience and perception of the problems of crime is valid and in no circumstances to be dismissed.

2 The victimisation of young people

Introduction

As we mentioned in the introduction, the results of the original pilot study in Craigmillar demonstrated that a very high proportion of young people had been the victims of offences against the person and of harassment, both by young people and by adults, in public places. Furthermore they suggested that criminal victimisation is a part of young people's lives which remains largely hidden from the adult world, that is both from parents and from the police.

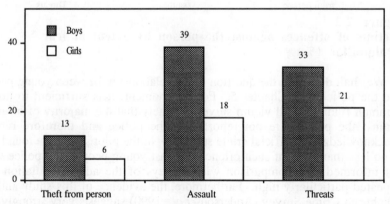

Figure 2.1
Victims of offences against the person - Craigmillar (%)

For example, young people in Craigmillar were asked whether, during the previous ten months: they had had something stolen from them, whether they had been hit or had force or violence used against them and whether they had been threatened. As Figure 2.1 shows, the results revealed high levels of personal crime, especially crimes of violence against boys.

The pilot study further suggested that much of this violence is relatively routine. For example, a third of victims of crimes of violence (assaults or threatening behaviour) had experienced such incidents on three or more occasions during the previous ten months. Although 75% of victims knew or recognised their assailant, 50% had been on their own when the last incident occurred. Thus, although such offences may be routine, as the graph below shows, one-third of victims reported that they had been 'very' or 'quite' frightened on the last occasion.

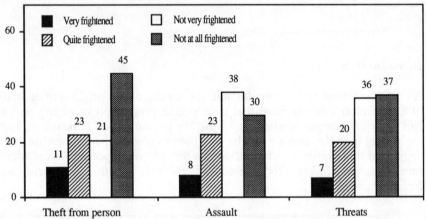

Figure 2.2
Victims of offences against the person by extent of fear - Craigmillar (%)

We shall deal with the question of the relationship between young people and the police in a Chapter 5. For the moment, it is sufficient to note a common finding in all victim surveys, namely that the majority of offences against the person are not reported to the police and therefore remain unacknowledged in official crime statistics. In the pilot study, we found that in no less than 83% of such offences against young people, the police were not informed. In comparison with surveys of the adult population this appeared particularly high. Furthermore, the evidence of this study and the Edinburgh Crime Survey (Anderson *et al.*, 1990) suggests very strongly that on many occasions young people are reluctant to tell their teachers and even their parents what has happened to them.

This reluctance is indicative of two themes which will be met repeatedly in this study: first, the ambivalence of young people towards towards adults in general and the police in particular; and secondly, the contradictory attitudes they hold in relation to their own victimisation.

This ambivalence raises a general point to be borne in mind throughout the following analysis as, for many young people, their own victimisation can prove to be a source of 'double trouble'. For example, very often in the interviews, young people would describe incidents such as kerb-crawling or indecent exposure, which had not been reported either to adults or to the police (although, importantly, they would have told their friends). Various reasons were given for this: they felt they would get into trouble 'because you shouldn't have been there in the first place'; some felt that they did not want to worry their parents and others that their parents might stop them going out with their friends.

Similar problems with under-reporting and the tendency to 'blame the victim' have been well documented in research on women as victims of crime, particularly in relation to sexual offences (Chambers and Millar, 1983). In relation to young people, however, it seems that adult responses to juvenile victimisation frequently lead young people to conceal the extent of their own victimisation. As we will see in the next chapter, the problems young people experience in this respect lead them to adopt a series of strategies aimed at securing their immediate self-protection and warning their friends about dangerous places, people and situations. Paradoxically, because these warnings are frequently conveyed in the form of myths or exaggerated stories, there is a tendency for adults to disbelieve them in their entirety and to dismiss young people's accounts of the world as 'childish nonsense'. As a result, the instances of victimisation and the level of fear it occasions remain even more invisible.

In terms of the law, the incidents so far described are all criminal offences. In terms of young people's lives, however, there are many other examples of general harassment, abuse and frightening and stressful events which may fall outside the law, but which contribute to general levels of anxiety and fear of crime. These were revealed in the pilot study, when respondents were asked whether they had been frightened by other young people and adults staring at them, asking them things, shouting or threatening them or following them by car or on foot. In relation to youth harassment, the graph below shows that, although this was more of a problem for girls than boys, the differences were not substantial. In total 76% of girls had been harassed by other young people in comparison with 70% of boys.

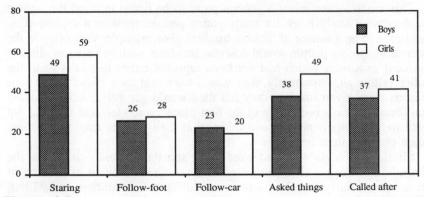

Figure 2.3
Victims of harassment by young people - Craigmillar (%)

The findings that gave us greatest cause for concern, however, were the incidents of harassment by adults, reported in total by 65% of girls and 53% of boys. The following graph again shows that the differences between boys and girls, with the exception of being stared at, were not very pronounced. Bearing in mind the lower rates of victimisation for theft, assault and threatening behaviour, such results suggest that girls are considerably more vulnerable to this type of problem, a question that we pursued in the subsequent interviews.

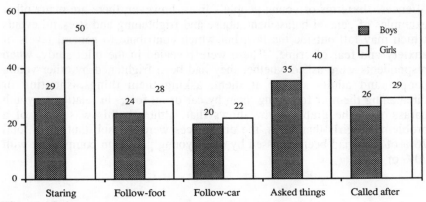

Figure 2.4
Victims of harassment by adults - Craigmillar (%)

When these results were followed up in interviews, we were provided with considerably more information about the nature and extent of victimisation than was covered in the questionnaire. For example, a number of the girls related how they had been frightened by men molesting or

38

sexually harassing them, suggesting that our questions on adult harassment needed to be expanded. The revised questionnaire for the main study therefore included more detailed questions on the time and location of the incident, the age of the wrongdoer, and whether or not the incident was reported to the police. In addition further questions were introduced asking both boys and girls whether they had been frightened by men 'trying to touch them', 'trying to get the young people to touch them', 'attempting to get them to go with them' and 'indecently exposing themselves (flashing).' The follow up questions were also included.

Young people as victims of crime

Offences against the person

The crimes examined in this chapter include offences against the person and harassment, both by young people and adults. In addition, we include the results on sexual importuning of both boys and girls by adult men. Following the findings of the pilot study, we shall give particular attention to offences committed by adults against young people. First, however, we shall examine offences against the person. These include: theft from the person, where something had been stolen directly from the victim with or without the use of violence; assault, where the young person had been hit or violence used with or without a weapon; and threatening behaviour where the victim had been threatened with violence.

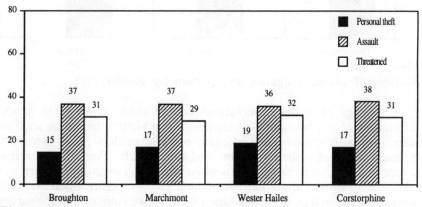

Figure 2.5
Victims of offences against the person (%)

In total, exactly half of the young people surveyed had been victims of one or more of these offences while in public places during the past nine months. Incidents occurring at home or in school were explicitly excluded.

39

In relation to theft from the person, a total of 17% of the young people studied reported that they had had something stolen from their person on at least one occasion in the previous nine months; 37% reported that they had been the victim of an assault at least once and 31% had been threatened with violence on one or more occasions. It can be seen from Figure 2.5 that there is extraordinary consistency in the findings across the schools.

This consistency is reinforced when the results are analysed by type of housing tenure. Thus, with victims of assault and theft from the person we find only a 3.5% difference between those who live in council houses (40% and 20.5% respectively) and those in owner-occupied accommodation (36.5% and 17%). In relation to threatening behaviour, there is a larger difference (34% to 29%) but again it is not substantial. However, as the following graph shows, the above figures mask the considerable differences between the proportion of girls and boys who have been victims of these types of crimes.

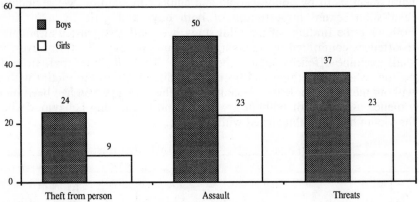

Figure 2.6
Victims of offences against the person by gender (%)

A number of initial observations can be made about these gender differences. First, boys are not only more often victims, but as we shall see later, they also commit such offences more often than girls. Secondly, different forms of violence may be used among girls. From the interviews it appeared that, on those occasions when girls resort to physical violence, it takes the form of pulling hair, scratching etc. - categories that were not adequately covered by the standardised question we employed in the survey. Thus, as the question referred to the victim being hit with 'fists or a weapon of any sort', the results are probably skewed towards typically male forms of violence. As some 14 year-old girls from Broughton explained:

40

A: I think that girls fighting is more vicious, I don't know how.

B: Girls fight a different way anyway. Claw your eyes out, pull your hair.

C: Aye boys jist start booting into you.

Moreover, girls may also employ other, less physical forms of violence. They ostracise the victim, engage in verbal fights, are rude to them and to others about them, and generally attempt to isolate them. This form of victimisation was not addressed in the questionnaire. For this and the above reason, the findings may not fully document the extent and impact of different forms of victimisation among girls.

But while receiving and giving 'burst noses', 'batterings' and 'paggering' other young people may be relatively commonplace - particularly among boys - we should stress that by no means all such incidents are restricted to their own peer group, nor that the impact of assault or threatening behaviour, upon either girls or boys, is in any sense trivial. As we shall see presently, such incidents are frequently disturbing and frightening. First, however, we shall look in more detail at the circumstances in which such incidents occur.

In the follow-up questions, we asked at what time of day or night the last such incident had occurred, whether the victim knew or recognised the offender and if they were alone at the time. All are of significance in determining the victim's feelings.

Table 2.1
Characteristics of offences against the person (%)

	Time of day		Know/recognise person		Alone at time	
	Before 6p.m.	After 6p.m.	Yes	No	Yes	No
Assault						
Boys	44	56	65	35	32	68
Girls	43	57	73	27	33	67
Threatening behaviour						
Boys	43	57	55	45	31	69
Girls	42	58	70	30	32	68
Theft from person						
Boys	68	32	41	59	32	68
Girls	40	60	59	41	33	68

From the above data it is noticeable that, in relation to both assault and threatening behaviour, girls were more likely than boys to know or recognise their assailant. Indeed, contrary to stereotypical images of boys fighting among their friends, in almost half the cases of threatening behaviour (45%), and in over a third of the cases of assault (35%), the boys neither knew nor recognised the offender. Two examples from Broughton demonstrate the gendered experience of assault. Two 14 year-old boys discussed the issue in the following terms:

A: A few weeks ago, someone who went to this school, in fourth year, he lives doon that way and he got jumped when he was on his way hame. They battered him, cracked his tooth, his face was all swollen. He had nothin tae dae wi fightin or anythin, he was jist on his way hame.

B: They take anyone.

By contrast, the girls understood the potential for becoming a victim of assault differently:

A: Depends if you've got a reputation for anything.

B: Depends if you've said something cheeky cos things get around.

C: It jist depends cos if there was a group of people and they said something to you and you jist told them to fuck off, then they would go, 'Right I'm going to kill you for that', because you were cheeky to them.

These accounts suggest that boys are more often the victims of gratuitous violence by strangers. However, as we will see in the next chapter such violence is more often a function of territory and where you live, rather than a product of personal disputes or arguments. Girls, on the other hand, have more direct contact with their assailant and the specific reason for the attack is more often known to them. Similarly with theft from the person the majority of the girls (59%) knew or recognised the offender, whereas this was the case for only 41% of the boys.

The number of victims for whom the assailant was a stranger seriously calls into question any assumption that such incidents are merely 'a bit of fooling about' between young male friends. A similar doubt arises when we look at the age of the offenders concerned. Thus, in less than half of the reported cases of threatening behaviour (43% of boys and 38% of girls) the offender was under 16. A further 46% of boys and 44% of girls had been threatened by someone aged 16 to 20. And, it is worth emphasising, 11% of boys and 18% of girls had been threatened by assailants they believed to be over 21.

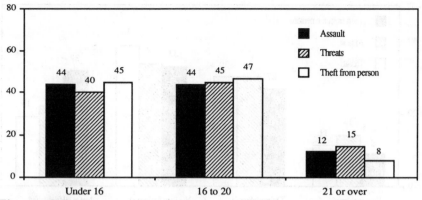

Figure 2.7
Offences against the person: age of offender (%)

A similar pattern is apparent in relation to assault. In less than half of the cases (43% of boys and 48% of girls) the offender was under 16; in 47% and 35% of cases the offender was aged 16 to 20; and in 10% of offences against boys and 17% of those against girls the assault was committed by someone over 21. In relation to theft from the person, 46% of offences against boys and 44% of those against girls were committed by offenders under 16; in 50% of offences against boys and 39% against girls the offender was aged 16 to 20; and in 5% of those against boys and 16% of those against girls the offender was over 21.

Thus, less than half the offences against the person are committed by other young people under 16. Such offences should not, therefore, be viewed solely as the product of peer rivalries. Indeed, 30% of threats, 27% of assaults and 21% of thefts from the person were committed by people aged 18 or over. We must, then, call into question the view that such offences refer solely to incidents among friends of the same age, and the cognate tendency to dismiss *all* such incidents as petty quarrels or youthful high spirits.

Such notions are further dispelled when we consider the next graph, which provides us with a broad picture of how frightening boys and girls found the incidents concerned. It will be noted that while the level of fear occasioned by assaults is very similar for girls and boys, in relation to threats girls express substantially more anxiety. Some 44% of boys said they had been 'very' or 'quite' frightened by assaults and 41% by threats. By contrast, 46% of girls had been frightened by assault and 56% by threatening behaviour. Conversely, a greater proportion of the boys who had been victims of theft from the person were 'very' or 'quite' frightened (35%) than girls (26%). It is perhaps surprising that girls did not register even higher levels of anxiety than they did, especially since girls experience these types of victimisation less frequently than boys.

43

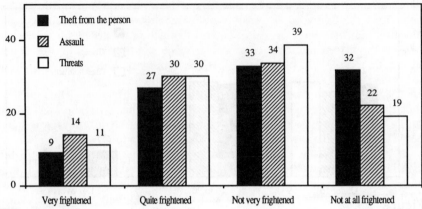

Figure 2.8
Male victims of offences against the person: extent of fear (%)

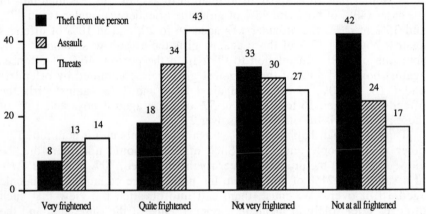

Figure 2.9
Female victims of offences against the person: extent of fear (%)

However, the above figures efface the extent to which the fear occasioned by the incident was dependent upon a combination of other circumstances over and above the gender of the victim. The most important of these were: (i) the age of the offender; (ii) whether the offender was a stranger, and (iii) whether the victims were on their own.

(i) Impact on the victim: the age of the offender. When we look at how frightened victims of assault or threatening behaviour were by reference to the age of the offender(s), we find the level of fear experienced is considerably higher when the assailant is 16 or older. Thus 37% of those assaulted by 10 to 15 year-olds reported that they were 'very' or 'quite' frightened; this rose to 48% in cases of assault by 16 to 20 year-olds and

63% for those assaulted by persons 21 or over. In relation to threatening behaviour, the figure of 41% of those threatened by 10 to 15 year-olds, who reported that they were 'very' or 'quite' frightened by the incident, rose to 57% of those threatened by 16 to 20 year-olds and 50% of those threatened by adults over 21. This general trend is replicated with victims of theft from the person, although the overall proportion of victims that were 'very' and 'quite' frightened is lower than for the other offences. Thus 20% of those robbed by someone aged 10 to 15 found the experience 'very' or 'quite' frightening, as did 43% of victims where the offender was aged between 16 and 20, and 39% of those victims of an adult over 21.

(ii) Impact on the victim: offence committed by stranger. Where the assailant was a stranger 58% of victims of assault, 53% of victims of threats and 42% of victims of theft from the person were 'very' or 'quite' frightened. This fell to 38%, 44% and 20% respectively where the victim 'knew or recognised' the offender.

(iii) Impact on the victim: victim alone. Similarly we find that 52% of victims of assault, 54% of victims of threatening behaviour and 45% of victims of theft from the person said they were 'very' or 'quite' frightened when they were on their own at the time of the offence. This compares with 41%, 44% and 27% of those who were in the company of others.

Such variables clearly compound one another. For example, in cases of assault where the victim was with others and knew or recognised the offender, one-third (34%) reported that they were 'very' or 'quite' frightened. This is still high but in sharp contrast with the two-thirds (64%) of those who did not know the offender and were alone at the time. Although our sample size is not sufficient to make a reliable statistical estimate, both the qualitative and the quantitative data suggest that these variables are compounded yet further by the gender of the victim so that, as might be expected, girls find such situations still more threatening than boys.

This heightened fear of strangers is demonstrated in the evasive action taken by the young people when they encounter others that they view as a threat. Thus as one 13 year-old boy at school in Marchmont explained:

> I used to deliver a paper and after about two months I gave it up because I didn't feel safe. I didn't actually see any of them *(casuals)* but I didn't feel safe in that area. I saw them like on street corners and I thought 'no this isn't going to be safe.'

Similarly, the girls were asked about their feelings towards 'casuals' they did not recognise ('casuals' are discussed in Chapter 4):

CS: Are you frightened by them?
A: Yes.

CS: *Do you avoid them?*
A: Automatically. I don't think about it.
B: If you see them in the street I just walk past them. If they
    see you avoiding them then they'll shout at you.
C: Never walk past them fast or with your head down.
(14 year-old girls, Marchmont)

We also looked at where offences against the person occurred. It was found that 14% of assaults occurred in town, 12% going to and from school, 34% elsewhere and 41% near home. Clearly, however, the significance of these figures depends upon the amount of time spent in these different locations. Thus, as the following graph indicates, many young people spend a considerable amount of time 'messing around near home', and it is not therefore surprising that the more time spent in this way the greater the likelihood of victimisation.

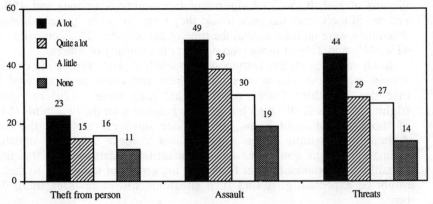

Figure 2.10
Victims of offences against the person by amount of time spent outside 'messing about near home' (%)

As a result, offences against the person most frequently occur near home and not, as is the case for adults, in other areas of the city such as the town centre. It thus becomes very important for young people to find ways of guaranteeing their security when out and about in their own area. As we shall see in the next chapter, one favoured way of doing so is collect together in groups and in 'gangs'. Ironically, the consequence of this is often further victimisation and harassment.

Harassment

In the last section, we looked at three specific offences which are clearly defined in the criminal law - namely, theft from the person, assault and threatening behaviour. In this section we examine types of behaviour which may be experienced as frightening and extremely unpleasant but may nonetheless fall outside the strict terms of the criminal law. Thus we included in the questionnaire a series of questions falling under the general heading of 'harassment'. The respondents were asked whether they had been frightened by people acting in any of the following ways: staring at you? following you on foot? following you in a car? asking you things? shouting at you or calling after you? threatening you? These questions were asked first in relation to harassment by 'other young people (about your age or a bit older or younger)', and secondly in relation to adults.

The experience of harassment by adults seems markedly different - and far more frightening - than that of being harassed by peers, simply because of the age difference. In recounting an incident where one of them had been followed by a man, a group of 14 year-old girls from Broughton conveyed this quite clearly:

A: He must have been about 18 or 19 he wasnae a ...
B: I don't think its so bad if they're young. It seems creepier if they're middle aged.

The pilot study from Craigmillar had suggested that for both boys and girls some of the behaviour described in our questions had more threatening, overtly sexual connotations when it concerned adults. One of the problems, therefore, in interpreting the results from these questions lies in untangling the different meanings attributed by the victim to such actions in different circumstances and in relation to different people. This is doubly difficult because we are dealing with a continuum of different types of behaviour, ranging from name calling to the possibility of kerb-crawling. In other words, these questions may be referring to overt sexual harassment or minor incivilities.

In one respect, however, this is unimportant - what matters is the impact the incident has on the victim. On the other hand, the findings strongly intimate that many such incidents, especially those concerning adults, actually amounted to sexual offences, or inchoate sexual offences as defined at law. For that reason, we included additional questions to establish the extent of sexual importuning. We should say, perhaps, that we were uncertain whether these questions would provoke excessive embarrassment or difficulty. In fact, for reasons that will soon become clear, both boys and girls answered the questions readily and without difficulty, and were often prepared to discuss the issues in the interviews.

It can be seen from Figure 2.11 that incidents of verbal and non-violent harassment by other young people are very common. In total two-thirds of the sample had experienced at least one such incident. Thus, 49% of boys and 44% of girls had been frightened by someone 'shouting' at them; 38% of boys and 44% of girls by someone 'staring' at them; 34% of boys and 30% of girls by people 'asking them things', while a large percentage of the boys were also threatened (42%). It is also noticeable that the marked gender differentiation, found in relation to the offences discussed in the last section, is not present. Indeed girls are as often victims of harassment as boys. This would appear to support our comments about the possible different forms that violence takes in relation to gender. However, as we said earlier, we need to undertake further research about the nature of violence experienced and employed by girls before we can draw any strong conclusions.

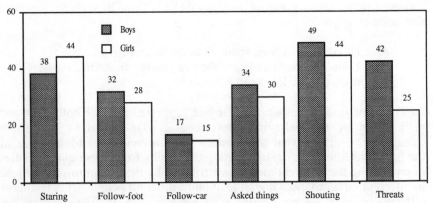

Figure 2.11
Victims of harassment by other young people (%)

When we analysed the incidence of youth harassment in the different schools we found that the pattern was broadly similar. In only one case was there a clear difference, namely the proportion of young people in Wester Hailes who said that they had been followed by young people in cars (23% boys and 22% girls) in comparison with those from Marchmont (16% boys, 8% girls). As the following graph shows, however, when the data is aggregated the rate of harassment is highest in Corstorphine, where, for example, 79% of girls had suffered one or other form of harassment, in comparison with 60% of girls from Broughton.

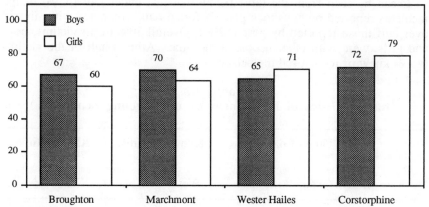

Figure 2.12
Victims of harassment by other young people by area (%)

It is not possible to determine why the figures for Corstorphine are consistently higher than elsewhere without a full analysis of local conditions. For present purposes what is important is the high level of harassment suffered by both boys and girls in all the schools.

When we look at where these incidents occurred, marked differences emerge between schools. Thus, for the total sample, the highest areas for harassment are 'near home' or 'elsewhere' (32% and 34% respectively), although nearly half of those from Wester Hailes who had been harassed (49%) reported that it happened 'near home'. For the young people from Broughton, however, these events more often took place 'in town' (35%) and 'elsewhere' (29%). This is probably a function of the proximity of the schools to the town centre.

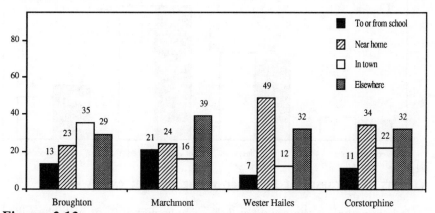

Figure 2.13
Harassment by other young people: where incident happened (%)

It can be seen from the table below that just under half (45%) of the incidents reported by boys took place before 6 p.m., compared with slightly over half those reported by girls (52%). Overall 50% of all victims, boys and girls, were with other people at the time. Around half of the victims (45%) knew or recognised the person.

Table 2.2
Characteristics of harassment by other young people (%)

	Time of day		Know/recognise person		Alone at time	
	Before 6p.m.	After 6p.m.	Yes	No	Yes	No
Boys	45	55	47	53	40	60
Girls	52	48	43	57	44	56

As we saw in relation to offences against the person, the particular circumstances of the incident determine how frightening it is. Thus 43% of those who were alone at the time, in comparison with 32% of those who were with others, described the event as 'very' or 'quite' frightening. In the majority of cases, however, harassment by other young people does not appear to cause much distress. As the following graph shows, over half of both boys and girls said they were either 'not very' frightened or 'not at all' frightened.

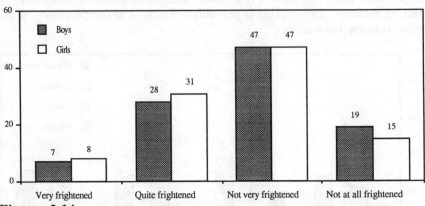

Figure 2.14
Victims of harassment by other young people: extent of fear (%)

It is nonetheless the case that 35% of boys and 39% of girls described such incidents as either 'very' or 'quite' frightening. We should again be

50

careful, therefore, not to downplay the level of anxiety occasioned or to dismiss such incidents in terms of 'childish rough-and-tumble'. Indeed, in Wester Hailes, nearly 50% of girls described the last incident as 'very' or 'quite' frightening. Furthermore, it should not be forgotten that our follow-up questions were addressed to 'the *last* occasion' on which they were harassed and as we have seen the majority of victims were not very frightened. However, had we asked whether the young person concerned had been 'very' or 'quite' frightened on *any* occasion during the recall period, undoubtedly a much higher proportion would have said yes.

Harassment by adults

Turning to the findings on adult harassment, we should reiterate our comment about the qualitative difference between harassment by young people and harassment by adults, and specifically that adult harassment may be associated with sexual harassment. This appears to be partly confirmed when we examine differences by gender. At this point it is worth remembering that when we looked at offences against the person, female victims were in the minority. In relation to harassment by young people it was noticeable that girls were equally as likely to be victims as boys. From the graph below, it is striking that girls now substantially outnumber boys.

According to the answers to the questionnaire, for the girls, the most common forms of adult harassment were being 'stared at' (32%), 'followed on foot' (27%) and 'asked things' (26%). For boys the most common were being 'asked things' (17%) and being 'threatened' (15%). Overall, some 52% of the girls had been harassed by an adult during the previous nine months as had 36% of boys.

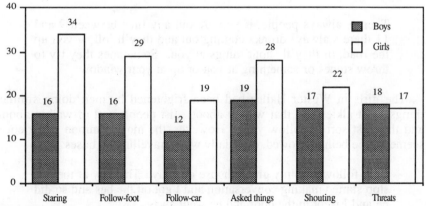

Figure 2.15
Victims of harassment by adults (%)

51

The findings obtained by the survey were strongly reinforced in the interviews with the young people, and it is pertinent to consider the examples that young people provided of harassment by adults. They can be divided into three main categories; in the first place, many young people feel anxious when they are out alone, as a 12 year-old boy from Broughton explained:

> It's jist at night sometimes you're a wee bit worried aboot adults and folk goin aboot . . . specially when its dark, ken, during the winter time.

The fear and experience of this seems to be heightened when it involves adults who have been drinking, as a 13 year-old girl from Marchmont commented:

> Sometimes if you're walking down the road and they're not very well lit streets it can get quite scary if they're coming out *(of the pub)*.

In a similar vein, the some of the girls reported having trouble with:

> A: Workies shouting things.
> B: Drunk men shouting for you to come over cos they want to speak to you.
> *(14 year-old girls, Broughton)*

Although these incidents occasion anxiety, others reported having experienced even more serious harassment in similar situations. For example, a 14 year-old girl from Marchmont complained that:

> There's always people, if you are out any time between 9 and 11 there's always drunks coming out and they'll follow you up the road, or they'll shout things at you. Sometimes they try to throw stones or something at you or up at your window.

The girls in Wester Hailes had been frightened by men doing similar things: 'Jist alkies and that walkin aboot. Jist people sort of walkin aboot and they jist sort of follow you.' However, the most common experience seemed to be being followed, especially when travelling on buses:

> I got followed to my gran's house one day. This guy at the bus stop started making conversation and I got on the bus and so did he and I went in the door and he went away.
> *(14 year-old girl, Corstorphine)*

Last week I was at the shows in Muirhoose and we got on the bus and this man got on. He had escaped from hospital cos he had hospital bands on each arm. And he started saying up yours and swearing at us, and we were telling him to shut up and swearing at him because he was swearing at us. And he said come here you, give us a kiss . . . to me. And I ran doon stairs, I was scared as anything and I just sat beside my pals. *(15 year-old girl, Wester Hailes)*

The extent of harassment by adults and the severity of the problem it causes to young people should not be underestimated. Furthermore, as the following graph indicates, it is one faced by young people in all the areas studied.

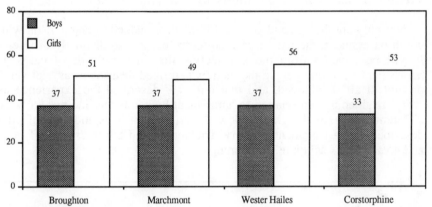

Figure 2.16
Victims of harassment by adults by area (%)

In terms of the age of the victims, there is again some difference in comparison with harassment by young people. In relation to the latter, we found harassment to be relatively evenly distributed among both boys and girls, but that, for both, the level of victimisation increases with age. With respect to adult harassment a slightly different pattern is apparent. As the next graph shows, there is a clear tendency for harassment of boys to decrease with age, while for girls there is a slight trend in the opposite direction. The full significance of this will become clear later, when we look at the findings on importuning.

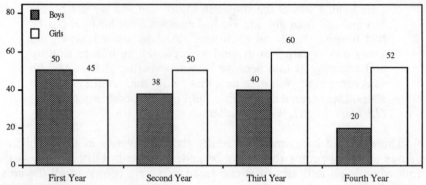

Figure 2.17
Victims of harassment by adults by school year (%)

Not only are the age and gender differentials marked in comparison with youth harassment, the pattern in relation to fear is also distinctly different. It will be recalled from the last section that in two-thirds of cases of harassment by young people the victims described themselves as 'not very' or 'not at all' frightened, and that only 7% described the experience as 'very' frightening. In relation to harassment by adults the findings are very different. Thus, as the graph below shows, 14% of boys and 25% of girls described the last incident as 'very' frightening and a further 36% of boys and 45% of girls as 'quite' frightening.

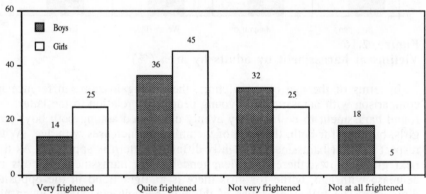

Figure 2.18
Victims of harassment by adults: extent of fear (%)

As with youth harassment, when we look at where the last incident occurred we find an uneven pattern. Among young people from Wester Hailes many more incidents occurred near home (52%), compared with young people from Marchmont (22%). Conversely, 33% of those from

54

Marchmont experienced adult harassment in town while the same was true for only 15% of those from Wester Hailes. Clearly, this is closely related to the amount of time young people spend in different parts of the city.

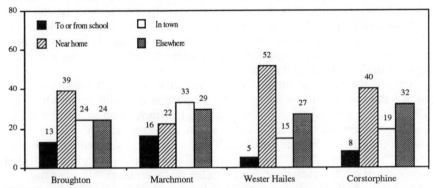

Figure 2.19
Harassment by adults: where incident happened (%)

When we looked at the incidence of different forms of harassment experienced by young people from the different areas, we found that among boys there was very little difference on all six measures.

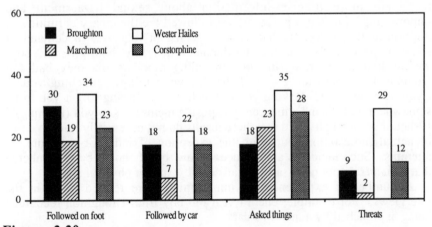

Figure 2.20
Female victims of harassment by adults by area (%)

Among girls, however, particularly in relation to the four categories shown in Figure 2.20, there was much greater variation. For example, while 7% of girls at the school in Marchmont had been followed by an adult in a car, 18% of girls from the schools in Broughton and Corstorphine and

22% of girls from Wester Hailes had experienced such problems. Perhaps most noticeable, however, is the very high proportion of those who reported having been verbally threatened in Wester Hailes (29%), compared with 12% from Corstorphine, 9% from Broughton and 2% of those at school in Marchmont. Again, it is difficult to assess why this should be the case without a detailed examination of local circumstances. For example, as we shall see in the next chapter, many girls living in Wester Hailes complained about harassment from 'junkies', a problem which, from the research, appears to be specific to that area.

One of the most important and distinct differences between youth and adult harassment is to be found in the proportion of incidents in which the offender was a stranger. It will be recalled that in relation to harassment by a young person the offender was known to, or recognised by, 47% of boys and 43% of girls. In relation to adult harassment this falls to 23% of boys and 17% of girls. In other words, in well over three quarters of all such incidents of adult harassment the offender was a stranger. Furthermore, in very nearly half of all cases (49% of boys, and 48% of girls) the person concerned was estimated by the victim to be aged between 30 and 50.

Importuning

Following the results of the pilot study in Craigmillar, we felt it necessary to obtain more precise information about sexual harassment and importuning. For these purposes, we followed the dictionary definition of importuning; namely, 'to harass with persistent requests; to demand of someone persistently.' In the questionnaire, therefore, both girls and boys were asked whether, during the preceding nine months they had felt frightened by men doing any of the following things: 'touching you or trying to touch you?' 'asking you to touch them?' 'trying to get you to go somewhere with them?' 'indecently exposing themselves to you (flashing)?' It should be re-emphasised that these results do not necessarily refer to cases of actual molestation, but, with the exception of indecent exposure, to attempts. Such incidents are offences at law, but it should be remembered that *attempts* do not necessarily entail actual sexual or physical abuse.

A number of experiences of importuning were related to us in the interviews. For example, one 14 year-old boy from Broughton recounted being approached by a man in a car:

> He goes 'Where's Redbrae's?' and he was right next to it. And I go 'Doon there' and he goes 'Can you get in the car and tell me?'

In a similar vein, a 15 year-old year girl from Corstorphine told us:

I was standing outside the pub waiting for my mum who was in the toilet and this man came up and said 'Do you want to go to bed?' I jist telt him where to go.

In total, 26% of the girls had experienced at least one of the above incidents in the preceding nine months. Although this is far greater than for boys, nonetheless 9% of young males had been similarly victimised. As the following graph shows, the most common incidents reported concerned cases of men trying to touch them (4% of boys and 17% of girls), and experiences of indecent exposure (4% of boys and 12% of girls).

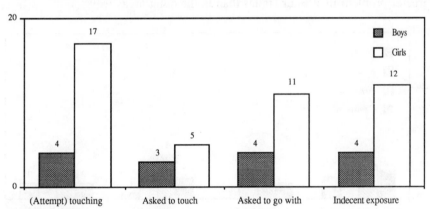

Figure 2.21
Victims of importuning by men (%)

When the aggregate findings were analysed by area, some differences appeared.

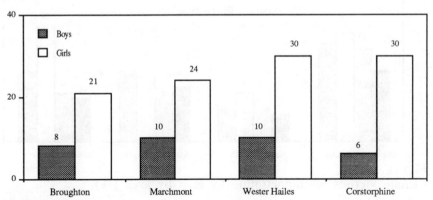

Figure 2.22
Victims of importuning by men by area (%)

Thus, as Figure 2.22 shows, 30% of girls from Corstorphine had been victimised as against 21% of those from Broughton. Such differences, however, are by no means as striking as the widespread distribution of this type of offence.

However, as the following two graphs indicate, such aggregate data masks the particular problems suffered by young people from the different areas. The findings for boys are broadly similar, with the exception of those at school in Marchmont, where a greater percentage (8%) reported men 'asking them to go somewhere with them' than at the other schools. Indecent exposure by men to girls is revealed by the second graph to be a greater problem in Wester Hailes than in the other areas.

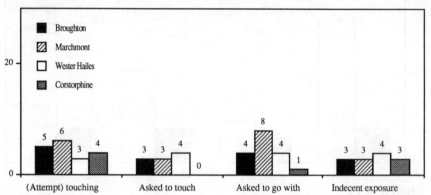

Figure 2.23
Male victims of importuning by men by area (%)

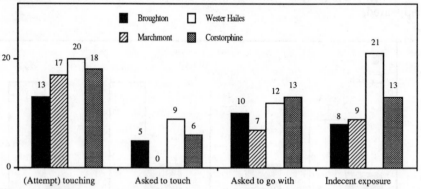

Figure 2.24
Female victims of importuning by men by area (%)

As we saw earlier in relation to harassment by adults, a very distinct pattern emerges when the age of victims of importuning is taken into account. Thus, as the graph below clearly shows, victimisation of boys tends to decrease with age. On the other hand, a different pattern is apparent in relation to girls; following a sharp increase between first and second years, the rate appears to stabilise at around 30%.

A further and marked difference from adult harassment is the higher proportion of girls who knew or recognised the offender. In relation to adult harassment we saw that this was the case in only 17% of cases, while in relation to importuning, no less than 40% of the girls 'knew or recognised' the person concerned. This is much higher than was found with boys (18%). The reasons for this, we believe, lie in the realms of adult sexuality and gender relations, and while such questions are beyond the scope of the present research, these broader issues require attention if an adequate understanding of such problems is to be reached.

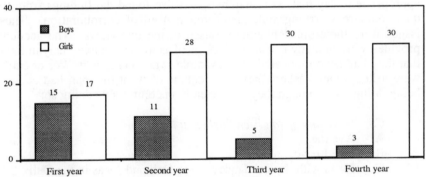

Figure 2.25
Victims of importuning by men by school year (%)

With regard to the age of the offender, 21% were estimated by the victim to be in their late teens; 28% between 20 and 29; 29% between 30 and 39, and 22% 40 or over. In so far as any assessment of age, such as this, can be reliable, it would appear that offenders are not restricted to any particular age group. Where the offender was known to the girl concerned (n=40), 47% were in their teens. By contrast, where the offender was a stranger (n=64), 71% were aged between 20 and 40.

Although the sample size is too small to be statistically reliable the data suggests that whether the man was known to, or recognised by, the victim varies according to the type of incident. Thus, in 60% of cases where the man had touched or tried to touch the girl (n=48), the offender was known to the victim. In 83% of cases of indecent exposure (n=35), and 78% of cases where the man had tried to get a girl to go with him (n=18), the assailant was a stranger.

Perhaps surprisingly, a slightly lower percentage of those who had been victims of importuning (55%) reported being 'very' or 'quite' frightened by the incident than those who had been victims of adult harassment (61%).

59

Among girls, however, this figure rises to 58% in relation to incidents where the offender was not known to them, significantly this figure rose to 66% in cases where they knew or recognised the person concerned.

We have seen that out of a total sample of 427 girls, 26% had experience of importuning. We have also seen that, on the most recent occasion, 40% knew or recognised the person concerned. On this basis, one in ten of our total sample of girls had been importuned by a man known to them, while more than one in six had been importuned by a stranger. When we take into account how frightening the incident was, we find that one in ten girls had been 'very' or 'quite' frightened by strangers importuning them (9.4%), while one in sixteen had been similarly frightened by someone known to them (6.4%).

We are aware that some people may be tempted to dispute these findings and question the credibility of what young people say. We think it appropriate to say that, as researchers, we also found the findings from the questionnaire worrying and, therefore, in need of corroboration. These issues were therefore deliberately raised in the interviews. The accounts provided were in many instances so detailed as to make it extremely unlikely that they had been fabricated. For example, when the girls in Wester Hailes were asked about flashers they gave details of what the man had actually being doing, even though they were clearly uncomfortable doing so:

CS: *Have any of you been flashed at then?*
A: Aye me.
B: Aye I have.
C: I was with my pal Tracey at the Dell and I was in the Dell water and naebody noticed him and when we noticed him he took his jacket off and he was standin there.
D: What was he doin, he wasn't flashin at yous though.
C: He was . . .
D: He was playin with his self right.
CS: *About how old was he?*
D: He looked like he was about 30.
(14 year-old girls, Wester Hailes)

What is more, so many (especially older) girls were familiar with the problem, and conscious of its extent, that we are left in little doubt as to the reliability of the responses to the questionnaire. Why such incidents should remain so hidden from public knowledge will be examined in the next chapter.

3 Living with crime

Introduction

We saw in the previous chapter that criminal victimisation is a common feature of many young people's lives. They have to come to terms with, and negotiate, a level of contact with crime that most adults would find intolerable. However, it is important to remember that they do not come into contact with crime only as victims. Their experience of crime is based not only on things that happen to them, but also on the things they see happening around them. Thus, if we are to understand fully the impact that crime has on the everyday lives of young people, it is also necessary to consider the question of how much crime they witness.

Although young people are frequently both victims of and witnesses to crime, as we shall also see, they seldom report such incidents to the police. Indeed, in many respects, young people live out their experiences of crime with little or no reference to the adult world. However, it is worth emphasising that for most young people, crime - though significant - is seldom allowed to dominate their lives. It might be said that while crime is everywhere, it is not everything. For while young people may not enlist the assistance of either the police or other adults, they develop their own strategies for coping with crime. Towards the end of this chapter we shall focus on these strategies in more detail. Before that, however, we look at the findings on both witnessing and reporting.

Crime is everywhere: witnessing crime

As can be seen from the following graph, the young people we interviewed had witnessed a considerable amount of crime across a range of different offences. However, five offences are witnessed far more frequently than the rest: namely, rowdiness, fighting, shoplifting, possession of an offensive weapon, and vandalism to property. In the questionnaire, we included a section in which we asked young people about their perceptions of the 'seriousness' of various offences. As we shall see in Chapter 4, these five offences are ones that young people themselves define as 'not very' serious.

Though many young people may not themselves think of these offences as serious, this does not mean that such offences do not have an effect on both their own and other people's lives. Indeed, as we suggest below, the 'minor' crime that young people see happening around them can have a considerable impact on their lives - both directly and indirectly. The sheer volume of incidents witnessed by young people seems to lead them to accept crime as an inevitable and everyday part of their existence, a fact that means they tend to both tolerate its presence and downplay its importance.

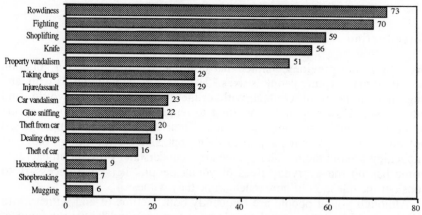

Figure 3.1
Witnessing of offences (%)

While young people most frequently witness what they term 'not very' serious offences, they also see a significant amount of 'very' serious crime. No less than 55% of the total sample had witnessed at least one crime involving either violence, drugs or dishonesty. For example, 31% had witnessed a serious crime of violence (deliberate injury/assault or mugging); 40% someone either buying, selling or taking drugs; and 21% a serious crime of dishonesty (housebreaking, shopbreaking or stealing a car). In the following graph, these figures are broken down by area.

It will be noted from Figure 3.2 that levels of witnessing are consistently higher among young people in Broughton and Wester Hailes than they are in either Corstorphine or Marchmont. Thus, for serious crimes as a whole, the highest figures are to be found in Broughton (61%) and Wester Hailes (60%), compared with 51% in Corstorphine and 48% in Marchmont.

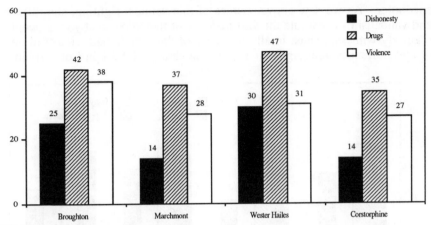

Figure 3.2
Witnessing of offences by area (%)

If we examine the data in terms of gender, we find that boys and girls witness very similar levels of serious crime.

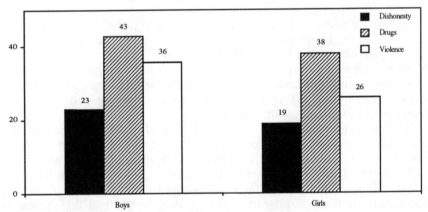

Figure 3.3
Witnessing of 'serious' offences by gender (%)

Thus, while 59% of boys had witnessed a crime they themselves perceived as 'very' serious, so had 51% of girls. The only difference of note concerned crimes of violence, which had been witnessed by 36% of boys compared with only 26% of girls. Despite these differences, it is obvious that young people generally witness what to adults must appear an alarming amount of 'very' serious crime.

While for a whole host of reasons the 'very' serious crimes that young people witness are important, so too are the less serious offences they encounter. As we saw above, crimes of this nature - fighting, shoplifting and vandalism - constitute the vast majority of the crimes that young people regularly witness. Thus, in all, over 87% of the sample had witnessed one of these offences, ranging from 83% in Marchmont to 89% in Corstorphine.

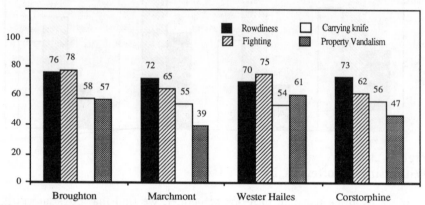

Figure 3.4
Witnessing of 'less serious' offences by area (%)

Across all areas then, the levels of witnessing of these offences are extremely high. Furthermore, the patterns we found in relation to the more serious offences are no longer evident. Instead, we find consistently high levels of witnessing of 'petty' offences, even in what are generally thought of as 'low crime-rate' areas, such as Corstorphine (Anderson *et al.*, 1990). It thus seems that this is a constant feature of young people's lives, regardless of the area in which they live.

The primary importance of these levels of witnessing lies in the cumulative effects of this degree of exposure to crime. For while seeing an isolated act of vandalism may be of little significance, repeatedly witnessing such 'minor' offences may contribute to a feeling of being surrounded by crime. Coming on top of their experiences as victims of crime and harassment, it is no surprise that many young people feel that 'crime is everywhere.'

This becomes apparent if we compare the amount of both serious and less serious crime young people witness with that witnessed by adults. Data from the Edinburgh Crime Survey (Anderson *et al.*, 1990) shows that, not only do young people experience far higher levels of victimisation than adults, they also witness far more crime. For example, during the *previous nine months* 59% of young people had witnessed somebody shoplifting, while *during the last five years* only 17% of adults had seen an incident of this nature. Similarly, 9% of young people had witnessed a housebreaking in the last nine months, compared to 6% of the adult population during the previous five years.

In many ways the higher levels of crime witnessed by young people are only to be expected. Young people generally spend more time out on the street and in other public places than do adults and, for this reason, are more likely to be in the places that offences are committed, at the times when they are committed. The table below shows the relationship between the amount of time spent on the street and the level of crime witnessed. Thus, for example, 51% of those who spent 'a lot' of time messing about or hanging around on the streets had witnessed a drugs-related offence, while this fell to 25% of those who spent 'none' of their time in this way.

Table 3.1

Offences witnessed by time spent 'messing about' outside (%)

Witnessed/Outside	A lot	Quite a lot	A little	None
Drugs	51	38	39	25
Violence	44	29	25	21
Dishonesty	33	19	15	12
Property vandalism	60	59	40	35
Carrying knife	68	58	51	38
Fighting	78	76	63	54

Though all this may seem obvious, it is of central importance. Throughout this study we have emphasised how the streets are contradictory places for young people. On the one hand, they are places where young people can generate their own fun, in relative freedom from adult supervision; on the other, they can be dangerous places where young people come into contact with crime as both victims and witnesses.

This brings us back to a key point made in the Introduction - that no single aspect of young people's contact with crime can be understood in isolation from the others. For young people, witnessing and victimisation are connected experiences - albeit ones of a different magnitude - which cannot be separated. They are bound up with one another for two essential reasons.

First of all, it may be that in some situations the witnessing of a crime may constitute, for the person seeing it, a form of victimisation. For example, a 'witness' of indecent exposure is clearly a victim, while the real 'victim' of a fight between two school friends may be the frightened bystander. Similarly, a young person who has seen someone carrying a knife, may feel vulnerable and anxious as a consequence. The point is that it is not only direct experience of victimisation which may cause people to fear for their safety. Witnessing crime can sometimes be sufficient *in and of itself* to heighten people's fears and influence their behaviour. As such, it adds an extra dimension to both their contact with crime, and to their perception of crime as a problem.

Secondly, it is quite simply the case that those young people who are most frequently the victims of crime are also the most likely to be witnesses of it. Across all offences, we found that those who had been victims of either harassment or personal crime were far more likely to have witnessed crime than were non-victims. For example, 71% of victims of serious offences against the person had also witnessed a serious crime, in comparison with only 33% of non-victims. This figure is broken down in the graph below.

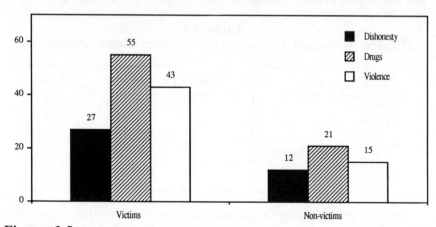

Figure 3.5
Witnessing of 'serious' crime by victims of offences against the person (%)

It would seem, therefore, that young people's experience of victimisation is frequently compounded by that of witnessing crime, to an extent that adults might well find intolerable. However, in evaluating the problem we should be careful to avoid tacitly imposing adult definitions and criteria. For, it is only through trying to understand young people's *own* views of their experiences as victims and witnesses that we can confront the problem in a way which will be both meaningful and acceptable to them: that is, in a manner which recognises both the reality of those experiences and the legitimacy of their strategies for dealing with them.

An important step in this direction is to consider the ways in which young people deal with their experiences of crime. For example, a typical 'adult' response might be to turn to the police. This might lead us to expect that, as young people are exposed to so much more crime than adults, so they would report more incidents, whether as victims or as witnesses. It is to this question - that of young people and reporting - that we now turn our attention.

66

Young people and reporting crime

Reporting by victims

Before looking in detail at the findings on the type of offences and the circumstances under which victims report crime to the police, we should make two basic but important points. First, it will be seen from the graph below that the levels of reporting are very low. For example, less than one in five (18.5%) cases of importuning and only 12% of cases of adult harassment are reported. This may appear surprising, given their relative seriousness and the level of anxiety we saw such incidents occasion in the last chapter. Secondly, we should note that even among the adult population, very few offences against the person are reported to the police. Thus, the Edinburgh Crime Survey found that just under one-third of assaults (31.7%); just over quarter of incidents involving threatening behaviour (27.6%) and slightly more than half of thefts from the person (55.7%) were reported (Anderson *et al.*, 1990:25).

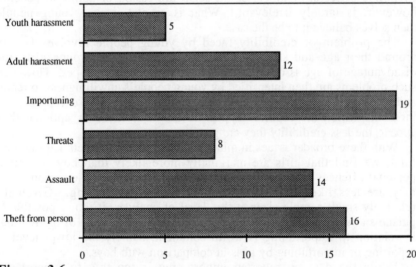

Figure 3.6
Reporting of incidents to the police (%)

However, the reticence to report found among young people has a special significance. For while, in some respects, the reasons why young people do not report may be similar to those given by adults (see Chapter 5), the wider consequences are different. First, the widespread failure of young people to report their victimisation effectively ensures that the problem remains hidden from official agencies and thus tends to be excluded from public debate. This is equally true of the under-reporting of certain offences

67

against adults - particularly in relation to domestic disputes and sexual harassment - which provide an illuminating parallel.

The Edinburgh Crime Survey, for example, found very high rates of harassment of young women by men - being kerb-crawled, followed on foot, verbally abused etc. Indeed, in some areas of the city, two-thirds of women between 16 and 30 had directly experienced harassment of this nature during the past twelve months. Despite the fact that the majority of women found such incidents frightening, over 90% decided not to report the incident to the police. As a result, sexual harassment of women remains one of the most difficult problems to deal with if only because there is so little official data on its prevalence.

We suggested in Chapter 1 that there is evidence that the attitudes of many of those working in the criminal justice system are informed by a paternalist conception of childhood which regards the evidence of young people with suspicion. In much the same way, other research has shown how women's testimony in relation to sexual assaults is discredited (Chambers and Millar, 1983). Whether or not such views are actually held by police officers, members of the legal profession or adults in general, however, is largely irrelevant. What is crucial is that young people themselves believe it to be the case.

The problem of credibility faced by young people revolves largely around their age and status as 'children' - although for young girls, the disadvantage of age is often exacerbated by gender stereotypes. However, such problems are then intensified by young people's unwillingness to report and a vicious circle sets in: the less that is reported, the more exceptional the incidents which are reported appear to be. The more exceptional they appear, the less credibility they are given.

With these broader issues in mind, we turn to the more detailed findings. First, we find that girls are marginally more likely than boys to report personal offences - that is, threats, assault and theft from the person - but they are less likely to report harassment and importuning. Given the relatively small sample sizes at this level of analysis, it is not possible to pursue statistical investigation further. However, one aspect of the findings in relation to importuning is worth comment, namely the lower level of reporting of importuning by girls in comparison with boys.

While the data on reported importuning is too thin to support any definitive conclusion, we suspect that in part the lower level of reporting by girls may be a consequence of their relationship to the offender. Thus, while 18% of boys said that on the last occasion of such an offence they knew or recognised the offender, this was true of 40% of offences committed against girls. In cases of importuning, therefore, it seems reasonable to suggest that when the offender is known or recognised, victims are more reluctant to report the offence.

68

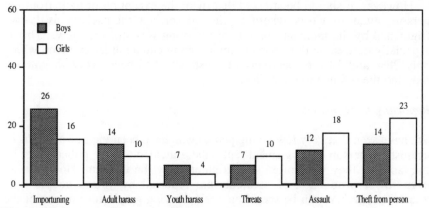

Figure 3.7
Reporting of incidents to the police by gender (%)

The question of the relationship of the victim to the offender and the decision to report is more complex than we have so far suggested. For while in the case of importuning knowledge of the offender appears to increase reluctance to report, in other cases the victim's lack of knowledge and, therefore, his or her inability to *identify* the offender may also influence the decision not to report. In such circumstances, the victim may well decide that there is little if any point in reporting the matter as there would be nothing the police could do.

A further factor which appears relevant to the decision to report victimisation is the impact of the incident upon the victim. Thus, as the following graph shows, 53% of victims of theft from the person who had been 'very' frightened reported the incident to the police in comparison with only 14% of those who had been 'quite' frightened.

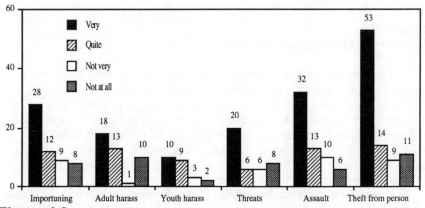

Figure 3.8
Reporting of incidents to the police by extent of fear (%)

69

However, it should be stressed that, with the exception of theft from the person, even in cases where victims described themselves as 'very' frightened by the incident, the rate of reporting was still very low. This is especially noticeable in relation to importuning and adult harassment, where only 28% and 18% respectively of those who had been 'very' frightened reported the offence to the police.

Reporting by witnesses

We have seen that very few young people who have been victims of offences against the person or harassment report these incidents to the police - despite the fact that they were often very frightened by the incident. However, an even lower proportion of incidents are reported by young people who witness crime. As can be seen from the following graph, for not one of the offences did more than a quarter of witnesses report what they had seen to the police. For the majority of offences, less than 10% did so.

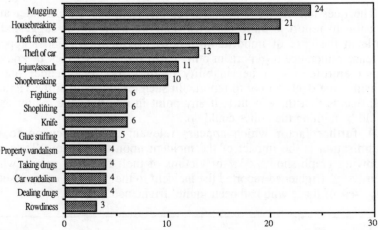

Figure 3.9
Witnesses reporting to the police (%)

It is noticeable that the offences young people report most often are those which they perceive as 'very' serious. However, given this perception, it is somewhat surprising that so few incidents of mugging, housebreaking and car theft are reported to the police. The proportion of drugs-related offences reported is even smaller, despite the fact that such offences were also classed as 'very' serious. Indeed, young people reported drugs-related offences no more often than they did vandalism and fighting in the street - offences they defined as 'not very' serious.

In comparison with the Edinburgh Crime Survey, as Figure 3.10 (based on Anderson *et al.*, 1990) shows, it is apparent that young people report

70

considerably less of what they see to the police than do adults. Thus, while only 21% of young people reported a housebreaking that they had witnessed, the same was true of 69% of adults. Similarly, 17% of young people reported a theft from a motor vehicle compared with 51% of adults.

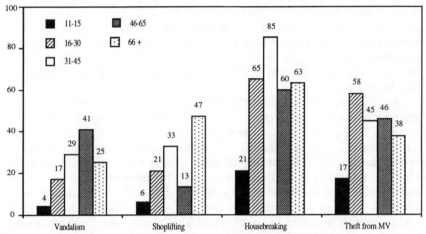

Figure 3.10
Offences witnessed and reported to the police by age (%)

For every offence witnessed, with the exception of 'mugging' (39%), the majority of young people knew or recognised the person or people concerned. For example, 84% of those who had seen somebody taking drugs knew or recognised those concerned. We find similar figures for buying and selling drugs (81%) and carrying a knife (81%).

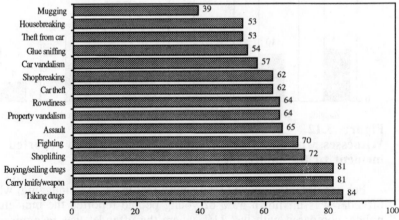

Figure 3.11
Witnesses who knew or recognised the offender(s) (%)

The relationship between the offender and a witness, like that of offender and victim, is a complex one. In the first place, the witness's ability simply to identify the offender may be a crucial variable in the decision to report. As important may be the *offender's* ability to identify the witness - in such instances, fear of reprisals may influence any decision. Over and above these particular issues, however, are more general questions about perceptions and values. For example, the witness's evaluation of the seriousness of the offence may be of greater or less significance in certain circumstances, as might be the attitudes of the witness towards the police. Finally, even more general considerations of loyalty to the peer group may also be at stake.

As we have stressed throughout this report, it is often of little help to attempt to analyse such questions separately or to suggest that any one variable is of greater significance than another. Later in the text, we shall have reason to suggest that one reason why young people do not report or 'grass' to the police is because to do so would reduce the protection from victimisation offered by their peers. For the moment, however, we shall merely note that in almost every case, but especially in relation to serious offences such as housebreaking, theft of a motor vehicle and mugging, young people are more likely to report an incident they have witnessed to the police where they did not know or recognise the offender.

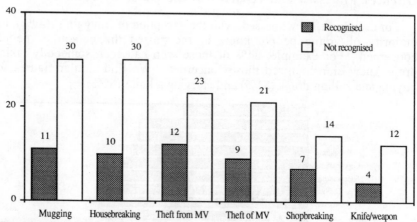

Figure 3.12
Witnesses who knew or recognised offender who reported incident to the police (%)

For example, the above graph shows that in cases of mugging, where the offender was unknown 30% of young people reported the incident to the police, compared with just 11% where the offender was recognised. This same pattern was found in relation to housebreaking, vehicle offences and shopbreaking - that is, in relation to crimes which young people identify as serious. Again, however, the most important point is the reluctance or failure to report even in those cases where there is no apparent relationship between the witness and the offender and in cases which young people themselves see as 'very' serious.

While most of the offences shown in the graph above are offences that young people tend to view as either 'very' or 'quite' serious, it is noticeable from the following table that the seriousness of the offence does not necessarily lead to its being reported even when the witness does not know the offender. This is particularly the case in relation to drug-related offences which, as we saw earlier, were among those offences most often perceived as 'very' serious.

Table 3.2
Witnesses who knew or recognised offender
who reported incident to the police (%)

% Reported to Police	Recognised	Not recognised
Injury/assault	12	12
Glue sniffing	6	5
Fighting	5	8
Shoplifting	5	8
Buy/sell drugs	4	4
Taking drugs	4	6
Rowdiness	2	3
Property vandalism	1	9
Car vandalism	1	7

The question of how young people decide to report an incident to the police or not is obviously a complex one. However, unless young people report offences, the police cannot be blamed for failure to act. However, as we shall see in more detail later, there was some evidence from the interviews we carried out with young people which suggested that, on occasions, the police do not treat young people's complaints with sufficient care. In this context, it is impossible to separate the reluctance of young people to report their contact with crime from the more general question of their relations with, and attitudes towards, the police. We will therefore delay discussion of these issues until we have looked in more detail at the issue of young people and policing (see Chapter 5). For the moment, we will merely say that, whether as victims or witnesses, young people report very few of the incidents they experience to the police and that they rarely use the police to assist them in dealing with their experience of crime.

It also seems that young people report very little of their contact with crime to adults in general. While we do not know from this study whether young people reported their experiences of crime to their parents, it would seem from the Edinburgh Crime Survey (Anderson *et al.*, 1990) that parents learn relatively little about offences committed against their children. In the crime survey, parents were asked whether their children had been victims of crime during the previous twelve months. While the two samples are not directly comparable (the Edinburgh Crime Survey asked about children aged between five and fifteen), in comparison with the findings on victimisation presented in Chapter 2, it would seem parental knowledge of their children's victimisation is slight.

Thus, while 37% of young people had been victims of assault, 31% had been threatened with violence and 17% had been victims of theft from the person, it would seem from the findings of the Edinburgh Crime Survey that parents are aware of only some of the offences committed against their children (over a recall period of twelve rather than nine months), as can be seen from the following graph.

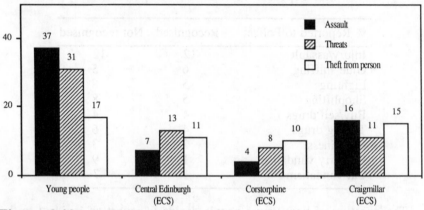

Figure 3.13
Victimisation of young people reported by parents (Edinburgh Crime Survey) and victimisation reported by young people themselves (%)

This would seem to confirm that young people live out their experience of crime with little or no reference to the adult world. In some ways this is not surprising. For, if young people are concerned to reduce the impact which their contact with crime has upon their lives, we should not expect them to go to the 'trouble' of reporting it to either an adult or the police. As we shall see below, it often makes more sense in these terms to attempt to deal with and manage the problem without resorting to outside help.

Crime isn't everything: fear of crime in context

From the findings presented so far we might expect the question of crime to be paramount in many young people's lives. However, when we look at crime and fear of crime in the context of young people's more general concerns, we find this is not the case. In the questionnaire, we asked young people whether they worried about a series of different issues, ranging from the family and school, to nuclear war and the environment, as well as crime. The results are presented in Figure 3.14.

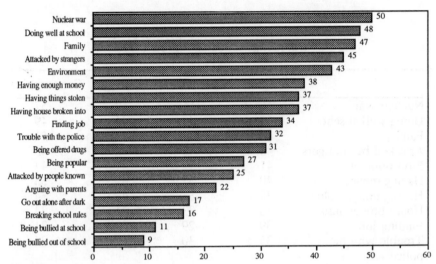

Figure 3.14
Young people worrying 'a lot' (%)

The question we asked gives no indication of why young people worry about these different issues. We are, however, able to draw some important conclusions about the *relative* importance of their different concerns. The first thing to note about the results is that, with the exception of 'being attacked by strangers', concern about crime ranks fairly low in the order of priorities. Thus, after 'nuclear war', young people worry most about their family and doing well at school. This perhaps should come as no great surprise as the school and the family are two of the most prominent aspects of any young person's life. However, it is worth reiterating the point made in Chapter 1 in relation to the 'underclass thesis' that there is little evidence to support claims that young people from deprived areas are disconnected or alienated from the conventional morality and aspirations of wider society.

This is not to say, however, that young people - whatever their background - do not worry about crime. As we can see, 45% of the sample worry 'a lot' about being attacked by strangers. Similarly, 37% worry 'a lot' about having things stolen from them. As we shall see below, this is particularly the case for girls. Indeed, being attacked by strangers is top of the girls list of worries - with 58% worrying about it 'a lot'.

In terms of the high levels of victimisation and witnessing we outlined above, it is difficult to regard these as anything but 'rational' fears. What is perhaps more surprising from an adult perspective is that young people place crime-related worries so low in their list of concerns - especially given their vulnerability to crime and the level of victimisation they actually suffer. In the table below, these figures are broken down by area.

Table 3.3
Worries and concerns: young people worrying 'a lot' by area (%)

	Broughton	Marchmont	W. Hailes	Corstorphine
Nuclear war	46	56	43	57
Doing well at school	57	43	44	49
Family	48	39	52	51
Attacked by strangers	45	42	44	48
Environment	41	52	31	47
Having money	40	32	42	38
Having things stolen	38	33	42	34
House broken into	38	33	41	34
Finding job	39	29	39	31
Trouble with the police	35	30	30	35
Offered drugs	34	22	36	31
Popularity with friends	25	28	21	35
Attacked by people known	28	22	25	24
Arguments with parents	21	20	25	21
Out alone after dark	19	17	15	19
Break school rules	18	13	18	13
Bullied at school	9	11	10	16
Bullied out of school	8	10	8	11

From this breakdown, we see that more young people in Wester Hailes worry more about more things than those living in other parts of the city. Thus, for eight of the eighteen issues, Wester Hailes scores highest. This compares with seven in Corstorphine, six in Broughton, and just one in Marchmont. For example, young people at Wester Hailes worry about their family and money more than young people in the other areas; and together

76

with those in Broughton they worry most about their future employment prospects. It is noticeable however, that those in Wester Hailes worry relatively less frequently about nuclear war and the environment.

It should also be noted that young people in Broughton and Wester Hailes are slightly more concerned about crime. Young people in the areas served by these two schools worry more about having things stolen, having their house broken into and being offered drugs than do those in either of the other two. However, the point we made above about these issues continues to hold. Across all four areas, crime-related worries do not figure particularly prominently on young people's list of concerns.

The contrast between boys and girls is much clearer than that between young people in different parts of the city. Girls worry more about all but one of the eighteen topics we asked about. Only on the question of breaking school rules do a higher percentage of boys say that they worry 'a lot' (16% of boys compared with 15% of girls). On all other issues girls tend to worry more, and in many cases substantially more so. For example, 55% of girls worry 'a lot' about their family, compared with only 41% of boys. The greatest gender differences, however, are found in relation to questions of personal safety. As the following graph indicates, girls worry far more than boys about being attacked (both by strangers and by people known to them), and about going out alone after dark. Given the rates of sexual harassment and importuning presented in the previous chapter, such concerns would seem justified.

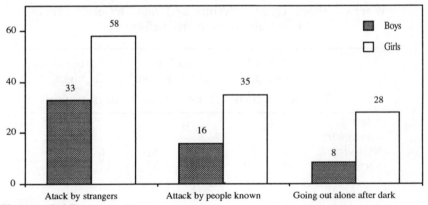

Figure 3.15
Young people worrying 'a lot' about personal safety by gender (%)

It would be a mistake though to assume that, because of their degree of contact with crime, young people's lives are dominated by a fear of it. Placed in a broader context, we can see that young people generally do not place crime-related worries at the top of their list of concerns. However, it

77

would equally be a mistake to assume that because young people report so little crime, that they do not care about it, or that it has no impact on their lives. It is clear, especially in the case of girls, that their worries about personal safety are both considerable and rational. This becomes apparent if we look at young people's worries in the context of their direct experience of crime.

If we look first at witnessing of crime, however, we find that it has a negligible effect on their levels of anxiety. Across the range of offences we asked about, we found no significant difference between witnesses and non-witnesses in terms of their worries about crime. For example, of those who had witnessed a crime of violence, fewer worried 'a lot' about being attacked by strangers (41%), than those who had not witnessed such an offence (46%). It may be, as we shall suggest below, that witnessing crime becomes an accepted part of their lives - something young people learn to live with.

However, the relationship between young people's worries and some forms of victimisation appears to be far stronger. This is particularly clear with regard to the different forms of harassment. We see from Table 3.4 below, for example, that while 64% of female victims of 'youth harassment' worry 'a lot' about being attacked by strangers, the same is true of only 43% of female non-victims - a pattern which is repeated for both adult harassment and for importuning.

Table 3.4
Worries about crime: victims and non-victims worrying 'a lot' about personal safety (%)

	Attack by strangers		Attack by persons known		Going out alone at night	
	Boys	Girls	Boys	Girls	Boys	Girls
Adult harassment						
Non-victim	29	51	14	31	6	23
Victim	39	63	19	38	11	31
Male importuning						
Non-victim	32	56	15	34	7	26
Victim	38	63	20	36	12	33
Youth harassment						
Non-victim	27	43	12	29	4	19
Victim	35	64	18	37	10	32

Two points can be made from the above findings: first, as we have already seen, the extent of girls' anxieties about crime exceeds that of boys; and second, that both boys and girls are more likely to worry about being attacked or going out alone at night if they have been the victims of harassment. In terms of other forms of victimisation however, this pattern is not so apparent. This suggests that it is the pervasiveness of different forms of harassment in young people's lives which is critical to their fears and anxieties about crime, rather than experience of particular offences such as theft or assault. It seems probable, although we cannot be sure, that the effect of offences against the person may be of a different quality in that they are 'over and done with' at the time. On the other hand, continued harassment perhaps contributes to lingering fears and a general sense of insecurity.

This suggests that previous discussions of fear of crime which have focused on whether or not it is 'rational' (Maxfield, 1984, 1988) have been wide of the mark. For example, it has been argued that women's fears of sexual assault are 'irrational' or 'unjustified' because the actual incidence of such offences is very low. However, as the Edinburgh Crime Survey (Anderson et al., 1990) showed, women are subjected to very high levels of sexual harassment and these experiences often occasion considerable anxiety about what might happen in the future - including more serious offences. In this context, we suggest it would be wrong to dismiss young people's fears and anxieties about crime.

The relatively low level of concern about crime expressed by young people must, in part, be attributed to a sense of resignation. Crime is, quite simply, something that young people have to live with and deal with when it happens. As the following accounts demonstrate, the philosophy which says 'don't worry about it until it happens' is laced with the expectation that sooner rather than later it will:

RK: *What worries you?*
A: I worry if I'm on mae own in the street. It's not that big but it's . . .
B: I was followed last week.
A: I've been followed loads of times. Loads. It's horrible, you dinnae worry so much like thinking if its gonna happen, but when it does honestly . . .
(13 year-old girls, Broughton)

CS: *Have you ever seen people committing crimes around here?*
All: Aye.
A: Breakin into cars and that, you see it all the time.
B: You jist get used to it.
(15 year-old girls, Wester Hailes)

Thus, while crime is often a concern for young people, they consign it to the back of their minds. They do so because it is important for them that crime does not unduly restrict their freedom and curtail their enjoyment. Indeed, in our interviews with young people, we found that they find their own ways of coming to terms with crime and lessening the impact it has upon their lives.

This situation is not difficult to comprehend since many adults experience similar problems. When we are outside, particularly if alone and/or at night, many of us feel anxious and worry that we will become the victim of crime (see Crawford *et al.*, 1990). However, this does not prevent us from going out either through necessity or for enjoyment. Thus, we find ways of dealing with our fears about crime in order to achieve some other goal. Similarly, young people manage their victimisation, and the threat of it because, on the whole, they enjoy being together and the freedoms that being outside offers.

Adults may travel in taxis, avoid certain places and go out with others, in order to minimise their risk of becoming a victim; young people utilise these and other techniques for the same reason. This does not usually involve a dramatic change in the way either group lives. However, because they are more at risk than adults, and do not - due to their status and economic position - have the same options, young people employ methods of trying to manage the problem of crime which are in many ways more subtle and sophisticated than those of adults. It is to these that we now turn.

Coping with crime

We have seen that young people tend to live out their experience of crime with relatively little reference to either adults or the police. In this section we look at the ways in which they deal with the problem of crime through reference to one another, in the context of their shared experiences. Like adults, young people talk about crime - about the particular things that have happened to them, about the things they see going on around them, and about the subject in general. Given its prevalence in their lives, it is hardly surprising that they find it an interesting topic of conversation. They tell each other 'good stories' - occasionally scary, sometimes funny, and often exaggerated. These stories frequently provide entertainment. But to dismiss them as 'kids' talk', based in a world of fantasy and invention, is to miss a very important point. For when young people talk about crime, their conversation is grounded in their genuine collective experience of it. They do tell 'good stories' - but for young people these stories are also a means of coping with crime.

Young people's talk about crime has different dimensions. In particular, we can identify two very common forms of discussing the issue. In the first place, they narrated personal accounts of incidents in which they had been victims or witnesses. Secondly, they told stories of extreme incidents, which did not necessarily involve either them or anyone they knew directly. These 'cautionary tales', as we refer to them, were often gruesome and exaggerated but they carried important warnings about potentially dangerous people, places and situations. The following is a personal account of a particularly troubling incident. It appeared that the young girl had been the victim of a sexual assault (she referred to it as rape) and she clearly felt uncomfortable recalling the incident. However, a friend prompted her until the full story was given by the two of them:

A: And she's been sort of raped before cos she was in the Clenzie. Ken it was a dump at the time but they've built workshops on it now. There used to be this big thing she was with some pals . . . *(Girl who was victim takes over)*

B: That's where we were and we seen this guy that said there were millions of sweets up there. He was only about 15 so we believed him. We were all goin in so I said 'I'll pass things oot to you.' So I went up there and they all ran away fae me and I was jist by masell and he raped me but I managed to get away.

A: No, he says. What was it he told you? To take doon your troosers, eh?

B: He pult his troosers doon first and said 'Pull your troosers doon,' and I said 'Nuh' and he turned away fae me and I kicked him in between the legs.

A: No but he threatened you as well and he said that and he said that if you didnae do it he was goin to throw you off the thing.

B: Aye he was goin to throw me off the wall but there was mattresses doon there anyway.

(14 year-old girls, Wester Hailes)

The accounts young people gave of their own victimisation were often very specific, although as in this example, sometimes the full details emerged only with prompting from others. This appears to demonstrate that these incidents had been discussed on previous occasions. In the example above, the victim obviously felt uncomfortable talking about her experience, but was able to do so because she had the support of her peers. Clearly, this kind of mutual support is an important part of dealing with victimisation. For young people, this is particularly important in the context of apparent adult indifference.

But accounts like this are also important at a more practical level. In the following two chapters, we will discuss in more detail the question of how young people learn the formal and informal 'rules' about crime and policing. Here, we will merely point out that the stories they tell one another about dangerous people, places and situations can be an important part of this process. In other words, they learn from their personal experience and from that of others simply by talking to each other about it. The following account of being kerb-crawled was given to us by a 13 year-old girl living in Broughton. It may be that none of the other girls in the group had been subjected to the same experience. Through her description of it, however, they will have learned a great deal:

> Ken, where Angie stays? You jist go right along and it's a bit creepy? I was just walking along an this guy kept on going in front of me wi his car an stopping till I walked past, then like I'd go further, then he'd go further than me. Then he'd stop until I walked past again an I thought 'Oh no'. I got to ma stair an I ran up the stair. I dinnae ken what he thought he was goin to do. He never got me anyway.

The above accounts are directly derived from personal experience. On the other hand, some 'cautionary tales' are closer to a type of urban myth (Brunvand, 1983). Frequently they relate to 'dangerous' places, like underpasses, or the lifts in the high-rise flats. The following example is taken from an interview with 13 year-old girls in Wester Hailes:

> I can't go up blocks of flats. I cannae, I'm scared of them. Wester Hailes or Clovey, I cannae remember which, and I went into a lift and there was blood all over the lift, ken at the top. Ma pal telt me this story - there was a man in the lift and the wifey walked in and he just sort of grabbed her when the lift was shutting and her heid got caught in it that's why there's blood all over it. There's a lot of murders in the high flats eh?

Shapland and Vagg (1988), among others, have suggested that stories such as this - myths about dangerous places in the city - become part of local folklore and more often than not bear no relation to reality. For example, in a discussion of a local park which was widely identified as unsafe, they concluded that:

Fear seemed to have more links with totems and folklore than with experience of or knowledge about criminal events. Perhaps this is not surprising. *Fear of crime, as opposed to concern about crime, seems not to be rooted in or tied to actual happenings.* Just as a phobia transcends its original cause so fear of the park had evolved far away from any initial reported incidents. It had become a place not to go to, a place populated by monsters - the modern equivalent to 'dragons live here' on medieval maps. (Shapland and Vagg, 1988:121; emphasis added)

We do not wish to take issue with Shapland and Vaggs' analysis of the particular park and its reputation. We would say, however, that the mythical stories told by the young people we interviewed about dangerous places, people and events *are* rooted - not necessarily in 'actual happenings' - but most certainly in their collective experience of crime. Their stories may not be true - that is, the incidents in question may never have happened, let alone to the young person recounting the story - but they still spring from, and feed back into, young people's real experiences. The story about the lift, for example, clearly *is* incredible, yet at the same time it speaks volumes about the experience of being a child in Wester Hailes. It is not the case, as Shapland and Vagg suggest, that fear almost always attaches to 'the unknown and the unusual' (i.e. to places which the person concerned never visits). The lifts - and their attendant dangers - are an everyday part of life in the high-rise flats on peripheral estates.

For this reason, we believe it is wrong to treat such accounts as symptomatic of an irrational fear of crime. Rather 'horror stories' of this type reinforce and add to the particular warnings young people pass on from aspects of their own lived experience. In the following example, a group of 12 year-old girls discuss the underpasses:

A: Over at Murrayburn in there's a little tunnel and some people always standing there and in there there's people . . . a person that rapes you.

CS: *A rapist? Is that in one of the underpasses? Do you think that is true? Do you think there is someone?*

A: Aye really.

C: Aye, I think so.

A: See in Sighthill there's a tunnel and you go under the tunnel and there's a big circle bit in between it and there's millions of people hang about there. And on the other side there's spray painting which says 'Make sure you die quickly' and drops of blood an that all over the walls.

These kind of stories are by no means limited to descriptions of dangerous places, however. We also heard several similarly exaggerated tales concerning people to be avoided. The following story, about a notorious local family, was recounted by a 13 year-old boy living in Marchmont:

> There's people that live down there, they're called the X's and everyone's scared of them. The wee-est X, he was getting dead cheeky to this big guy and the big guy was about to hit him and X's dad came out with a pick-axe and put it through the guy's knee. If they're at the park then we just go back home.

The exaggeration apparent in the above stories adds interest to them. But it also helps ensure they - and their message - travel. Thus, whether or not the story is true is relatively unimportant, as is whether or not the young people actually believe it. What is important is that the ideas contained within it are relayed to all concerned. Here is another example from Wester Hailes:

> (I hate) the quarry cos there is people that go roond with screw drivers and they catch a cat and they put a screwdriver through its heid and all that. That's what they do in the quarry and sometimes they throw them in the canal and sometimes they just leave them lying.
> *(13 year-old boy, Wester Hailes)*

The important point about conversations such as this is that they are not simply random expressions of 'childish imagination'. Like the discourse of adults, though probably more so when it comes to crime, young people's discourse is anchored in real experience. At one level, the above accounts are just stories - but at another, they reflect many young people's experience of crime and provide a means of coping with it. It is in this latter sense that they are important, for they represent a response to actual victimisation - and a way of dealing with very genuine and routine problems.

'Culture of defence'

Some commentators on youth culture have described the styles and activities of young people in terms of 'resistance through rituals' (Hall and Jefferson, 1976) - a form of expressive rebellion against a political, economic and social system which is systematically loaded against young people. While this approach has some value, in our view many of the 'troublesome' activities young people engage in are better read in terms of a 'culture of defence' characterised - above all else - by a loyalty towards one's peers as a form of protection.

Thus, although young people cope with crime by talking to one another about it, they also employ more concrete strategies. In a very practical way, they use each other - 'hanging around' in groups for protection. There are a number of reasons for this. Clearly, hanging around outside with your friends, away from adult supervision, is good fun. But as we have already seen, the streets and other public places carry risks for young people, as it is here that they come up against crime. Repeatedly we were told how being part of a group gave young people a sense of security. The following example, from an interview with 13 year-old girls at Wester Hailes, is typical:

A: Well you feel safer with a gang cos you never ken who's goin to jump oot on ya.

B: When I'm oot with a couple of lassies I'm still scared. But when I'm oot really late with loads of laddies and lassies I feel safer.

Ironically, however, it seems that part of the reason young people hang around together is that they are afraid of victimisation by other 'gangs'. In other words, the 'gang' is both a source of security and of potential trouble. As one 13 year-old boy from Corstorphine told us:

I go aboot in groups so other groups dinnae come after you. If I'm mysel and a group chases me I jist go up tae ma bit and get a group fae there and go doon. They'll no chase me again when I'm on my ane - I'll jist get ma pals.

The same point was made by a 15 year-old boy from Corstorphine:

That's why you hang about in groups. So if someone beats you up, you've got someone else to beat them up.

Thus, young people form gangs partly as a means of coping with victimisation, and partly for its own sake - as a source of fun. However, a large group of young people will often be seen by adults as a source of nuisance or even a threat - factors which can occasion adults calling the police. As a result, the means of dealing with trouble, often leads to trouble from the police (see Chapter 5) as well as trouble from young people living in different parts of the city (see Chapter 4). For the moment however, we shall concentrate on the mutual protection such strategies provide, the ground rules they impose and the histories upon which they draw.

The 'defence mechanisms' young people employ can take any or all of the forms we have already described: mutual support and sympathy, 'cautionary tales', and collective self-defence by associating in groups. These strategies, we suggest, reinforce one another. For example, a 'good' story as well as conveying warnings, can circulate among young people as a means of confirming the status of being an 'insider', thereby strengthening the solidarity of the group. Crucial in this regard, is the notion of loyalty.

Loyalty to 'folk from your own bit' was a constant refrain among the young people we spoke to. This phenomena can only be fully understood in terms of the history of the city (and perhaps other Scottish cities) and the spatial relations which this imposes upon the present generation. In Edinburgh, because of the extreme spatial segregation we described in Chapter 1, this *may* be of greater significance than elsewhere. For example, it seems that the 'casuals' (discussed at greater length in the next chapter) are a particularly Scottish phenomena, which in Edinburgh have become as much to do with 'territory' as they have with football. Thus, in a city where areas have such a distinct history and character, it is crucial for young people to know both their area and the dangers it holds (the function of 'cautionary tales') and to be able to rely upon other young people for mutual support (the function of groups) - especially when, as we have seen, levels of victimisation are so high.

However, as we shall see in Chapter 5, when we look at the reasons why young people report so little of their contact with crime to the police, 'loyalty' has a further, more immediate reference point. This relates both to the history and concept of childhood and the status of young people *vis-à-vis* the adult world. Thus, a second, and very powerful, refrain was consistently heard throughout the interviews: namely, the injunction against 'telling tales' and 'grassing'.

Like childhood itself, 'telling tales' has a history. For example, Aries describes how the early system of school monitors in British public schools - in which pupils were appointed to inform on the extra curricula activities of their classmates - came to be frowned upon and abolished during the 19th century. (Aries, 1962:246-254). 'Sneaking' came to be viewed as behaviour 'unbecoming' to a prospective 'officer and a gentlemen' - not only contemptible but bad for morale and discipline. This same deep-seated cultural disdain for 'telling tales', we would suggest, can still be encountered among some parents and teachers today. However, in the context of childhood, 'telling tales' has a self-evident double meaning, for not only is it wrong to tell tales, the tales themselves are probably wrong and not to be believed.

In addition to the twin possibilities of either being sanctioned for sneaking or being disbelieved (or very possibly both), there is another, very important, reason why young people prefer to with cope with crime by themselves - the fear of 'double trouble'. For example, telling parents about victimisation can often lead to 'sanctions' which further curtail freedom - such as not being allowed out. Alternatively, complaints to the police may

86

result in a generalised police response against *all* young people, as occurred in the now notorious 'Swamp '81' operation that sparked the Brixton riots.

From all points of view, therefore, it makes more sense for young people to rely on their friends and 'safety in numbers' - a strategy that is put at risk by 'grassing' to the adult world, for it may result in exclusion from the very group that offers young people protection. It is this point that concerns us here. For, given the amount of crime young people experience both as witnesses, and more seriously, as victims, exclusion from the group as a 'grass', a 'sneak' or a 'tell tale' can only result in heightened vulnerability to and fear of crime. The following account - from a group of 15 year-old boys in Corstorphine - affords a perfect example of what it is like to 'live with crime' in such a way:

A: I've got this guy, big guy, he's left school now. He's always bothering me. He goes down the way when I'm doing my papers. And I had my Drifter *(name of bike)* and I went into one of the hooses and he threw it in a burn, and the wheel was all smashed. The next day he asked me for a paper and I wouldnae give him one, so he punched me in the face a beauty. And the next time I was goin down the lane and I never even noticed him and he punched me in the face, and I went right through this hedge and landed on my arse. He hassles me all the time. Whenever I see him I just go 'Oh no!' and I walk the other way.

SA: Does it really bother you?

A: Aye, it does sometimes. When I go home I'm upset about it. Usually I've got a big lump on my head.

SA: Do you tell anyone about it?

A: Well, I never told anyone the first time. The second time he punched me a real beauty and I went home and I couldnae really disguise it - you know this big swelling mark on my right eye. And my dad went, 'Oh I'll phone the police, I'll phone the police' and that, but I didnae want that.

SA: Why not?

A: Didnae want any hassle.

B: If you press charges he'll be after you cos you pressed charges.

A: And if he gets put in jail, then his pals'll come after you. It's a vicious circle.

C: Just get people who can go after him. That's what I'd do.

A: But I dinnae know anyone that's hard enough.

C: Well unlucky then!

4 Breaking the law, learning the rules

Introduction

> MARCH OF THE MINI THUGS
> Teeny thugs have chalked up an all time record for violence in
> Scotland. There's been a massive 24% rise in serious crime
> among kids. The number of kids reported for serious assaults
> in 1988 was 280 - Up 54 on the previous year and DOUBLE
> the 1980 figure. (*Daily Record*, 12 July 1990)

Bad as they may seem, these figures cannot be taken seriously. They are a
ridiculous *understatement*. First, of course, they are based only upon
incidents which are reported to the police and, as we have seen from our
findings on victimisation and witnessing, a very large proportion of crime is
never reported to the police at all. Secondly, the figures refer only to
incidents in which the police identified the offender, that is, where the crime
had been cleared up. Again, as a proportion of crimes reported, those
cleared up are only a small fraction. Not surprisingly, therefore, the least
change in public reporting practices, especially if combined with greater
police attention to such cases, may result in an a substantial increase in the
official figures.

This process runs the danger of being accelerated as the results of studies
such as our own become available. As such studies become more reliable,
so claims which highlight the 'growing problem of juvenile delinquency'
appear to be justified. We have, therefore, several concerns in presenting
our findings here. First, our figures reveal that the extent of youth
offending is considerably higher than the official figures suggest. This is
inevitable given the nature of police statistics. However, the level of
offending should not, in our view, be allowed to become the stuff of
exaggerated headlines. Indeed, the damage that would done to young people

were this to happen would, in our view, far exceed the damage done by young people themselves.

Secondly, we are concerned that the findings should be placed carefully within the context of the experiences young people encounter and the definitions they employ, rather than in terms of the legal and moral categories employed by those who deal with them as offenders. In particular, we shall see that the young people who commit offences hold views on crime which are far removed from the stereotypical portrait of the predatory or mindless thug (Kinsey and Loader, 1990).

Third, while recognising the social costs and individual harm that youth crime occasions to the population at large, it is essential that these findings are placed within the costs to the young people themselves, that is in the context of their own victimisation and their quality of life. For example, the offences which the young people commit almost inevitably place barriers between themselves and the police and thus reduce the likelihood of their reporting or going to the police or other adults for help.

Finally, we want to insist that for the most part youth crime - especially petty offending - is best understood as a transitory event rather than a symptom of any underlying commitment to delinquent values (Matza, 1964). At this point we should also stress that, it was not the object of this study to analyse in detail the specific conditions which promote repeat offending among young people. This is not a study of juvenile delinquency *per se*. Rather, our topic is the broader issue of how young people come to understand crime and the criminal justice system through their contact with the police and their experience as victims and witnesses as well as through offending. In that context, we are looking at offending as part of a broader process through which young people come to terms with the formal and informal rules which govern their lives.

In this chapter, we shall begin by looking at patterns of offending by young people. This will include an analysis of specific serious offences; namely, crimes of violence, drug-related offences and serious crimes of dishonesty such as housebreaking and car theft, after which we shall examine what are generally regarded as 'petty' offences and 'incivilities' such as vandalism and rowdiness in the street.

We will then look at some more popular explanations of 'delinquency' - at the attitudes and social values of those who commit offences as well as the social background and the environmental factors which may or may not be relevant.

Patterns of offending

To establish patterns of offending, young people were asked the following question: 'Since the beginning of the last summer holidays, when you have been out near where you live have you ever done any of the things mentioned in the list?' The list included the following fifteen offences and misdemeanours:

Deliberately damaged a parked car or van?
Deliberately damaged buildings or public property?
Been rowdy or rude to people in the street?
Sniffed glue?
Fought in the street?
Deliberately injured or assaulted someone?
Stolen a car/van etc?

Stolen something from a shop?
Carried a knife or weapon?
Broken into a house ? (including attempts)
Broken into a shop ? (including attempts)
Mugged someone in the street?
Bought or sold illegal drugs?
Taken illegal drugs?
Broken into a car/van etc. (including attempts)?

In total, we found that, during the nine months immediately preceding the survey, 69% of young people had committed at least one of these offences on one or more occasions. The percentage of young people committing the different offences is shown below.

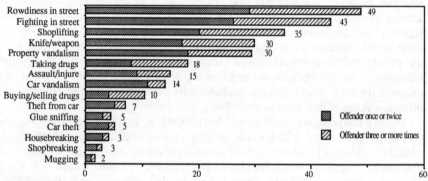

Figure 4.1
Young people committing offences (%)

The finding that seven out of ten young people in our sample had committed at least one of the 15 offences or incivilities (rowdiness and fighting) during the nine month period shows how widespread youthful offending is. Thus 72% of young people from Broughton, 62% from Marchmont, 76% from Wester Hailes and 68% of young people from Corstorphine had committed at least one the above offences in the past nine months. In no sense, therefore, can 'delinquency' be regarded as the preserve of any particular group or section of young people. On the contrary, rule breaking and petty crime would seem to be very much a

90

normal feature of young people's lives, wherever they come from and whichever school they go to.

It might be felt that the inclusion of rowdiness and fighting in the street unduly distorts the above findings on the grounds that such 'incivilities' do not necessarily constitute criminal offences. We would point out, however, that the Chief Constable of Lothian and Borders Police has included the maintenance of 'public tranquillity' as the first of six primary objectives for the Force in 1990. This includes the reduction of anti-social behaviour on the streets and for this reason and in relation to the findings from the Edinburgh Crime Survey (Anderson *et al.*, 1990) we chose to include these categories. If we exclude rowdiness and fighting in the street we find that 57% of the total sample had committed at least one of the 13 *criminal* offences in the last nine months.

'Serious' and 'less serious' offences

When we asked respondents to rank the above offences in terms of their 'seriousness', a very substantial majority of the sample identified eight of the fifteen listed offences as 'very' serious. These were: car theft (76%), glue-sniffing (76%), shopbreaking (81%), taking drugs (81%), causing deliberate injury/assault (82%), housebreaking (85%), buying or selling drugs (85%) and mugging (88%). For the purpose of the following analysis, these have been classified as 'serious' offences. The remainder we refer to as 'less' serious offences.

Overall, we found that 27% of the sample had committed at least one serious offence during the last nine months. Furthermore 16% had done so on three or more occasions. This latter figure, however, is heavily skewed by the relatively high proportion of drug-related crime and by the number of assaults respondents had committed. Thus, the number of young people committing three or more offences such as mugging, housebreaking, shopbreaking and car theft is relatively small. This means, of course, that it is not possible to undertake any detailed analysis of these particular crimes.

To overcome this problem and for the sake of brevity, therefore, the data on serious offences have been aggregated into three general categories: (i) *serious property crime*, composed of car theft, shopbreaking and housebreaking; (ii) *serious drug-related offences*, in which we have included glue-sniffing as well as taking illegal drugs and buying or selling illegal drugs; (iii) *serious violent crime*, including causing injury/assault and mugging. The reader should bear in mind, therefore, that these categories are necessarily rather coarse, particularly with regard to the last mentioned which really reflects only one offence, namely deliberate injury/assault. Where sample sizes allow, particular offences are analysed in more detail below.

From the following graph, it will be seen that the rate of serious offending at Wester Hailes is consistently higher than the other three areas. However, to maintain a proper perspective, it is probably more appropriate to stress that, at Wester Hailes as in the other areas, a majority of young people (65%) had committed *none* of these offences.

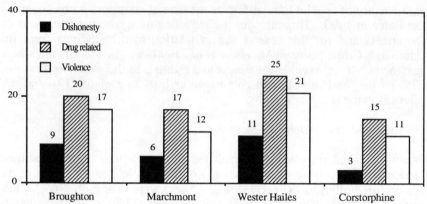

Figure 4.2
Young people committing 'serious' offences by area (%)

As the next graph shows, however, much stronger differences emerge when the data are analysed by gender.

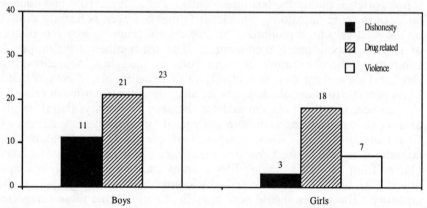

Figure 4.3
Young people committing 'serious' offences by gender (%)

However, as we mentioned earlier in relation to victimisation, it may well be inappropriate to read too much into the differences between girls and boys in relation to violent offences, as girls may well engage in

92

different *forms* of violence. Nonetheless, it remains the case that almost a quarter of the boys (23%) surveyed had committed at least one violent offence during the previous nine months, though it should be noted that these were predominantly assaults causing injury rather than mugging, which had been committed by only 3% of the boys. Similarly, considerably more boys (11%) than girls (3%) had committed serious property crimes. In comparison, however, the rate of drug-related offences among boys and girls was very similar.

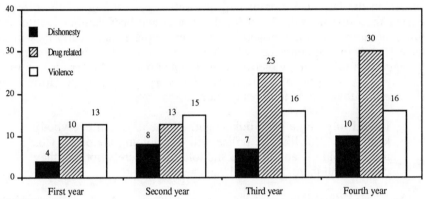

Figure 4.4
Young people committing 'serious' offences by school year (%)

As the last graph shows, the age breakdown for serious offences reveals a distinct pattern in relation to drug-related offences but not in relation to the other two categories. Thus, drug offending accelerates markedly from first year to fourth year at school. In first year 10% had committed at least one such offence in the past nine months. By second year this rose to 13%, by third year to 25%, while among fourth years 30% had committed such offences. In contrast, crimes of violence are very evenly distributed, while serious property crimes show a more gradual increase with age - 4% of first years, 8% and 7% of second and third years and 10% of fourth years.

Deliberate injury/assault

The interviews we conducted strongly suggest that a large majority of incidents described in this section occurred in fights between boys of the approximately same age, particularly between rival groups of 'casuals'. Nonetheless, it is should be noted that the questionnaire distinguished between 'fighting in the street' and 'deliberately assaulting or injuring someone' and that respondents had already evaluated these offences in terms of their seriousness. Thus we found that 57% of boys reported that they had

93

been involved in fights, while less than half of that number (23%) had actually 'deliberately injured or assaulted someone' during the past nine months. The incidents reported and analysed in this section relate to this latter category and are therefore 'serious' (and perceived to be so by the participants) and should not, therefore, be dismissed in terms of 'boys will be boys.'

From the results in the last section and those in the previous chapter, it is clear that violence and the threat of violence among and between young people is commonplace. Indeed, 69% of those who had committed an assault in the last nine months had themselves been victim of the offence during the same period. Even for those who had been neither victim nor offender during this time, violence is so commonplace that clearly they must have friends or acquaintances who had been victims. It is by no means an exaggeration to say that violence is an accepted part of life, for girls as well as boys. A 13 year-old girl from Wester Hailes made the following statement with an air of total resignation:

> I ken I'm going a get a doin, right? Some day. An everybody kens that. But like the police will dae nothing aboot it. Cos they've told me and told me and told me. There's nothing they can dae and there's nothing I can dae but take it.

As we saw in the last chapter, protection from violence depends much upon familiarity with your area and being known 'in your ain bit'. Moving home, for example, can thus prove difficult: 'When you first get there, mebbe for the first couple of years, you might get battered by the tough nuts and all that, but after a couple of years they'll get used to you and they'll no touch you. And if other people don't know you, the people that you do know'll tell them not to touch you. I used to get battered regularly. Mebbe sometimes I'd come home with a black eye, a thick ear.'

The reasons for such violence are varied but, as these statements show, its prevalence is taken for granted. The assertion of individual power and personal reputation is one factor. As one girl from Corstorphine put it: 'Some folk just like to stir up trouble an that. They just want to think they're smart. They want to be better than you.' In a similar context, a 14 year-old girl from Leith described an incident involving her friend:

> There is this girl who thinks she is really hard and Sally was a bit cheeky to her. The other girl went around saying things about her and she was up the town with some pals one day and she saw Sally and battered her. She only did it cos she was up the town, she didn't think that anybody would stop her, she just jumped her.

94

On other occasions, the reputation of the school may be decisive. The boys from Marchmont were currently confident of their own status, thus: 'The other school's got much more *(casuals)*. None that would do anything to us, cos they know we're in Marchmont.'

Through the interviews, it emerged that the 'casuals' figure prominently in the lives of young people throughout Edinburgh, indeed much more so than we initially realised. While stories were told about older 'casuals' - the 'heavies' or the 'big boys' - being involved in serious crimes such as drug dealing and shop-breaking, the younger people we interviewed gave no evidence to support the stereotypical representations commonly advanced in the press of 'highly organised gangs' of young people dedicated to 'irrational violence'. Certainly, the young people referred repeatedly to 'the Elite', 'the Hibs Baby Crew', 'the CCS' (Capital City Service) the 'Wester Hailes Soccer Club' etc. And it is understandable how the media images are constructed when young people in Broughton refer to 'the heavies in the Elite' and to themselves as being in the 'Elite Nappy Crew' (for 11 to 12 year-olds) and the 'Elite Baby Crew (for 13 to 15 year-olds).

Such terms could suggest a sophisticated system of recruitment, initiation and leadership. Indeed, many police officers we spoke to in the course of related research were convinced that the 'casuals' represent a sinister departure from previous forms of youth culture. Just as stories and urban myths circulate among young people, so too the same stories were relayed to us by police officers. Proceeds from street robberies and theft were said to be pooled to pay fines. The 'casuals' go on 'military-style exercises' along Princes Street before staging fights with the police. The leaders use cell-phones to deploy their troops (Kinsey, 1992).

Clearly we are not in a position to dispute the content or accuracy of police information (we understand a separate 'casuals' register' is held by police criminal intelligence). However, in relation to the young people we interviewed, we found the 'casuals' to represent a complex mix of myth and reality, security and ritual with little, if any, formal organisation. Between 11 and 15 at least, the different 'crews' refer to a very loose network - indeed, a casual association - based on school or area rather than a sinister organisation or gang.

This is not to dispute the reality of the aggression and violence expressed towards boys from different neighbourhoods. The following extract is typical:

A: If Trinity sometimes comes doon and starts making trouble - see, if they come doon and batter say, one laddy on his ane, that's what starts it.

B: We dinnae like Trinity, you've got to understand that. We fight them all the time. We pagger them. Every night.

C: I know, like if we were living down there, like at Trinity then we'd be used to walking aboot there cos we'd ken

everybody there just like we ken everybody here. We'd
be safe walkin aboot.
(14 year-old boys, Broughton)

If the term should be used at all, 'membership' is signified by a style of
dress and mode of behaviour. Thus a 'casual' is someone who 'dresses
barrie, barrie at fightin and everything'; who has 'expensive clathes and
likes to cause trouble'; 'who goes around in a group, tries to be hard; hangs
around on street corners' or who 'batters people for no reason.' For some -
a minority - the 'casuals' symbolise qualities of masculinity, toughness etc.
which are to be admired. (Though it would be wrong to see 'being a casual'
as an exclusively male privilege - girls also refer to themselves as
'casualettes'.)

For the majority, however, feelings about the 'casuals' were more
contradictory. Thus, most of those we interviewed distanced themselves
from the 'casuals' - they were too often a source of trouble. *En masse*, the
'casuals' could be threatening, while to be identified as a 'casual' by the
police was a guarantee of trouble of a different sort. However, such views
were frequently tempered by a level of realism, frequently absent from the
more lurid accounts of the popular press. As one girl said:

A lot of them, if you get them on their own they're really nice.
But then you get them together. They're all horrible, well
they're not all horrible but they're not nice if you meet them in
groups.
(13 year-old girl, Marchmont)

Yet the loose network of local 'casuals' can also offer a sense of security
and a form of informal protection, whether or not the dress and the style
was followed. Thus, for some 'going aboot in groups' was seen to be a
necessity in order to protect themselves, especially if they were to venture
out of their own territory and even if it meant storing up troubles for the
future. One 14 year-old boy from Broughton summed up the situation as
follows:

I go aboot in groups so other groups don't come after you. If
you're aboot yoursell groups come after you, if I'm masell and
a group chases me I jist go up to ma bit and get a group fae
there and go doon. They'll no chase me again when I'm on my
ain I'll just get ma pals.

Thus, for some, the 'casuals' are 'trouble', for some they're 'barrie', for
some they're just 'wee raj casuals'. For others, they provide security; for
others they can provide a genuine sense of excitement - albeit of a
contradictory kind: 'There's big excitement after school. Yeah, there's a

fight, let's go and see it.' 'I don't like it but you have to go. You feel a bit shocked.' The following accounts bring a number of common themes together:

> There's nae youth clubs in this area, right? Up there . . . up there at the church there's one but it's crap cos all the big laddies are being cheeky, you know. So you muck aboot in the park and you're moved by the polis. You muck aboot at Claremont Court and you're moved on by the polis. You go back to St. Mark's park and you get moved on by the polis. What dae they want us a dae? Muck aboot up the toon an get mugged? So, you've got tae stick together. We wouldnae dae anything, ken? But, you'd be frightened, wouldn't ya? If you was walking through the park an you saw mebbe thirty or forty of us together? But what are we supposed to dae?
> *(13 year-old girl, Marchmont)*

> Ken, it's good. We've got a really healthy crew since we joined up wi Trinity. Ken, we mebbe go fightin an all. But we're no thiefs. I mean, they wouldnae dare go up to an innocent person just walking along the street and say 'You', know what I mean? Like they all say we're goin to steal old grannies' bags an that. Who do they think we are? They do! We're no like that, we're no thiefs . . . I mean it's good. A whole bunch of us. It's just exciting being together. Ken?
> *(14 year-old girl, Broughton)*

This element of fun should not be under-estimated. For young people do not form groups solely for protection. Being part of the group is one important way in which they make their own entertainment and have fun. Thus, in the interviews, young people from all over the city would consistently link street fighting and the excitement it generates to the lack of alternatives: 'We done that *(went for a fight)* oot of boredom. We had nothin tae dae so we went doon lookin for a fight . . . go doon tae Broomie. That's the nearest place. That's all.' Girls in Wester Hailes, who had themselves been involved in fights, argued: 'If we had a place tae go and that and somebody said "Let's go doon fightin" we'd say "jist stay here" Somethin tae dae here instead of lookin for trouble.' Girls at Marchmont had much the same idea: 'Casuals and skaters both go around beating people up. Only skaters have other things to do with their time too, whereas casuals don't so they fight more.'

In many instances, young people described 'organised' fights between rival 'casuals' from different areas. However, from what we were told, it seemed they were treated more like ritual or seasonal events, characterised by their symbolic rather than actual violence. Indeed, even when an individual finds him or herself alone, encounters with 'casuals' from other areas do not necessarily lead to violence. As one boy said, 'They might give you a chase for fun like, if they catch you they don't hurt you or anything, they just go "ha, ha we got you".' Someone from Broughton described such ritualised events as follows: 'They arrange fights between other groups and they get there and both face each other and then they all run away. One group chases the other and they go back.' Her friend added: 'It's just like a game of chasey. Its really, really silly.'

However, while such rituals may provide excitement and establish collective loyalties, it should be stressed that a substantial proportion of boys reported that they had actually been attacked 'because of where they come from in Edinburgh.' This was most pronounced in Wester Hailes (17%) and in Broughton (13%), though boys at the school in Marchmont (8%) and those from Corstorphine (7%) also reported such incidents. (In contrast, out of the total sample, only 2% of girls reported this kind of attack.)

These findings point to the double bind in which young people can very easily find themselves. 'Going aboot in groups' can provide protection for young people but it may also provoke others and thus increase their vulnerability, especially when they are alone. Likewise adults may define such activities as threatening and make complaints to the police. What begins, therefore, as a source of excitement and security can thus provoke trouble from the police and as well as further violence. This vicious circle can take a further twist, of course, when young people start carrying weapons.

Carrying knives and weapons

As we saw earlier, in total some 30% of the young people we surveyed had carried knives or weapons on at least one occasion during the previous nine months. Of these, 17% reported having carried knives on one or two occasions while 13% had done so on three or more occasions.

These figures are substantially above official police statistics. In 1989, for example, Lothian and Borders Police reported only 584 cases of carrying an offensive weapon of which 583 were cleared up. Such cases are most often 'made known' to the police following the exercise of specific powers of stop and search and are, again, necessarily a substantial under-estimation of the actual level of the offence. However, our experience from discussing the findings from the pilot study at a recent conference of the Scottish Association for the Study of Delinquency suggests that some senior police officers may be tempted to dismiss such 'academic' findings as 'out of touch' with reality according to the police. Again, therefore, the discrepancy between official police statistics and our findings requires careful interpretation.

The pilot study had suggested two main characteristics of the problem. First, although carrying weapons was relatively common among a substantial minority of young people in Craigmillar, it was also relatively infrequent and restricted to particular circumstances. It should not be assumed that young people are automatically carrying knives simply to appear tough. Thus secondly, as a rule weapons were carried 'defensively' rather than 'offensively'. Typically, girls would carry a weapon when out alone (even in their own area) for self-defence against men. For boys, on the other hand, carrying weapons was usually restricted to occasions when they went 'up the toon' or ventured into areas where they felt unsafe. To put this in context, it is useful to remember that the Edinburgh Crime Survey found that 15% of women between 16 and 30 carried some means of self-defence (Anderson et al., 1990:38).

In the follow-up research therefore, it was necessary to establish, first, whether carrying weapons was a form of behaviour specific to young people in Craigmillar; and, secondly, if it was not, whether young people from other areas put forward similar justifications for doing so. As we have seen already, the findings were not unique to Craigmillar. Significantly, the following graph shows how remarkably consistent the findings were across the four areas studied. Thus the proportion of boys who had carried a knife or weapon during the previous nine months was virtually identical across areas (the greatest difference was between the areas was 3%). Very similar findings were obtained from girls in three of the areas - 17% in Broughton, 21% Wester Hailes, 20% Corstorphine. In Marchmont, however, the figure for girls fell to 8%.

At present, we are unable to offer a specific explanation for this disparity, as it would appear that it is most likely a product of specific local and cultural conditions. For example, adjacent to Marchmont are the Meadows - an area with a reputation throughout Edinburgh for offences against women. Thus, a number of girls from this part of Edinburgh reported that their parents would not allow them to take paper rounds in the evenings because of their worries about sexual assault. In other areas, however, where parents are perhaps less aware of the incidence of, for example, sexual harassment and importuning, a number of the girls we interviewed said they would carry a knife or weapon when out alone at night.

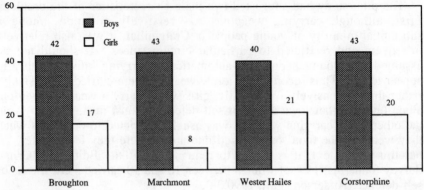

Figure 4.5
Young people carrying of knife or weapon by area and gender (%)

As in the pilot study, we were informed that carrying 'offensive' rather than 'defensive' weapons was relatively infrequent but, nonetheless, violence and talk about violence is a widely accepted part of young people's lives. Thus very similar stories circulate - especially among boys - in very different parts of the city. However, almost without exception, these stories are relayed at second-hand and relate to incidents occurring in other areas - if they occurred at all. The following extracts are typical of boys talking about violence:

> Some people carry knives and that. They started a fight and the guy that was from Longstone got slashed all the way down there. *(showed throat)*
> *(13 year-old boy, Wester Hailes)*

> There was a Broomhouse boy and about six Saughton jumped oot a van wi golf clubs and the Broomhouse laddie was in intensive care for about three months.
> *(14 year-old girl, Wester Hailes)*

> Aye. Somebody from Wester Hailes got killed up here. That's how there's always fights cos Wester Hailes think that we'll never be even with them till we've killed one of their boys.
> *(13 year-old boy, Wester Hailes)*

> See Broomie killed one of our boys from up here, so it's jist been fightin since then. That's how it all started.
> *(13 year-old boy, Wester Hailes)*

In so far as these accounts clearly carry warnings, they can be seen as 'cautionary tales' gone wrong. Whereas the stories referred to in Chapter 3 - such as the tale about the woman murdered in the lift - carry injunctions to stay away from certain places and people, these stories tend to exacerbate anxiety and to encourage the carrying of weapons. Furthermore, newspaper reports - such as that referred to above under the headline 'March of the Mini-Thugs' - may well serve to underwrite the popular myths of the playground and the street corner. Indeed, it may well be that an unintended consequence of the recent campaign highlighting violent crime in Edinburgh has been to reinforce if not create a 'moral panic' among young people in the city (Home Office, 1989). On the other hand, as the above extracts also reveal, such perceptions have been left by and inherited from previous generations and traditions - 'Mental Drylaw', for example, still lives on in the memory of older residents of Leith and Edinburgh.

Ultimately, however, we again come back to the deeper history of the Edinburgh, and the extreme spatial and social segregation which that history reveals and confirms in the 'territories' young people inhabit. Similarly, it must be recognised that the expectation that 'boys will be boys' and the tacit acceptance of male violence which such views condone, leave young males in a position where they are thrown back on their own resources - another instance of the fragmentation of the concept of childhood.

Thus, even in his early teens, a boy is expected to 'be a man' - not to tell tales, to stand up for himself, to learn to fight his own fights etc. But then, as we have seen, contradictions set in. For adults living in the area, groups of young people are seen as threatening, complaints are made to the police and young people become an object *of* policing. As we shall see in detail later, the needs of young people *for* the police thus become obscured and frequently hidden from official knowledge.

Drug-related offences

Out of the total sample, some 21% of boys and 18% of girls had committed at least one drug-related offence during the last nine months. In this section we shall look in more detail at how these figures break down in relation to the three offences included under this general category - namely, 'taking illegal drugs', 'buying or selling illegal drugs' and 'glue-sniffing'.

We noted earlier that there was a general tendency for contact with illegal drugs to increase with age. The following table shows the data on taking drugs analysed by school year. It can be seen that while 5% of young people in the first year had taken illegal drugs on one or more occasions, this rises consistently through second and third years so that by the fourth year some 29% of young people had tried drugs at least once; of these over half (58%) had done so on three or more occasions. In terms of gender

101

there was no appreciable difference, thus 18% of boys and 17% of the girls had taken illegal drugs within the last nine months.

Table 4.1
Use of illegal drugs by school year (%)

	First	Second	Third	Fourth
Never	95	90	75	72
Once	3	1	9	8
Twice	1	2	1	4
Three or more	1	7	15	17

As the next table shows, a very similar pattern is revealed in relation to buying or selling drugs, although this is not as widespread as actual consumption. Thus while 3% of first years had bought or sold drugs, this rises steadily through second and third year to 15% in the fourth. Again there is a very clear tendency to repeat the offence, with 62% of those who had committed the offence doing so on three or more occasions. In total, 13% of boys and 8% of girls had bought or sold drugs at least once during the nine month period.

Table 4.2
Bought or sold drugs by school year (%)

	First	Second	Third	Fourth
Never	97	91	85	85
Once	2	2	4	3
Twice	1	2	1	3
Three or more	1	5	10	10

When these findings were analysed by reference to area, quite strong differences emerged, particularly in relation to repeat offending. This is most obvious in relation to consumption where 16% of the young people in Wester Hailes had taken drugs on three or more occasions in comparison with 3% in Corstorphine. The following graphs show the percentage of those who had taken drugs on either one or two occasions and those who had done so three or more times.

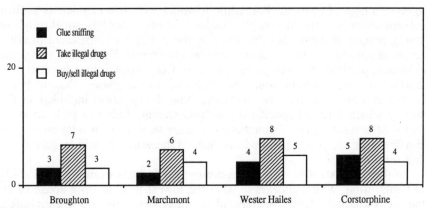

Figure 4.6
Young people committing drugs offences once or twice by area (%)

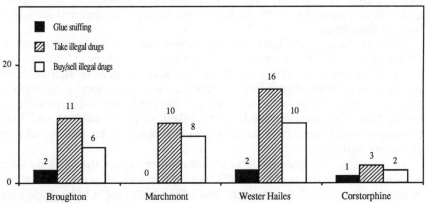

Figure 4.7
Young people committing drugs offences three times or more by area (%)

The comparison between Corstorphine and Wester Hailes is striking. However it should not be allowed to distract attention from what appears to be a relatively high level of drug use among young people throughout the city, especially those in their third and fourth year at school. Thus in Marchmont, 17% of fourth years had used illegal drugs on three or more occasions, as had 19% from Broughton and 23% of young people in Wester Hailes and 8% in Corstorphine.

An equally striking feature of these results is comparatively low level of glue sniffing. While we believe these particular findings may be significant in the longer term and offer some pointers for future policy, we ought first

103

to enter a note of caution. For, while it would seem that campaigns against solvent abuse in general and glue sniffing in particular has got through to young people, it seems that this form of abuse may been displaced to other forms of solvent and to soft drugs, such as marijuana. Thus, there was some evidence, particularly from young people in Corstorphine that although glue sniffing is comparatively rare, other forms of solvent abuse - 'buzzin gas' - is still common. It may be, therefore, that the question included in the survey which referred specifically to glue sniffing failed to pick up other forms of solvent abuse. Nonetheless, it does seem that, in relation to glue sniffing at least, young people have heeded the warnings and largely avoid this form of abuse.

In this context, it is worth considering the findings from the pilot study in Craigmillar, which appears to have the lowest level of drug abuse of all the areas studied. Unfortunately, in the pilot study, we did not include a direct question on consumption, however, as in the other four areas, the young people were asked whether they had bought or sold drugs. Two per cent had done on one or two occasions and only 1% three or more times. This is clearly substantially lower than in any other area and on first sight is all the more surprising, given the reputation the area has acquired for a high level of drug abuse.

From the face to face interviews we carried out with the young people in Craigmillar, we were strongly convinced that the survey findings had provided an accurate reflection of the low level of drug-related offences among young people in the area and that the message of local campaigns in the community and in the school had got through to the young people. In which case, the question needs to be asked why the national and local campaigns should have been so successful in Craigmillar but not, apparently, elsewhere in the city?

In our view, this question is in urgent need of further study, as we were unable to explore the matter in sufficient detail. Indeed, it may be that use of certain drugs - such as marijuana and LSD which appear to be those most widely available to and used by young people in the other four areas - has increased at Craigmillar since the pilot was undertaken In the view of the headteacher at the school in Craigmillar, however, the situation has not changed and drug abuse is still comparatively rare among the young people in the area.

Tentatively, therefore, we would suggest that the difference lies in the particular history and structure of the local community. In comparison with more wealthier areas of the city, Craigmillar is a geographically defined and contained community, in which the problems of drug abuse are well known, as too are the drug users themselves (in the Edinburgh Crime Survey 57% of the Craigmillar population described drug abuse and drug dealing as a 'big problem in their area' - Anderson et al., 1990:11). The headteacher described the situation as follows:

Children here do actually see the drug community. I think the drug community in Craigmillar is probably different in character. In Craigmillar, as far as I know, there is a defined drug community - it's a tighter community, they hide from the police but they do not seem to hide from the community particularly, they are known to the community. They are secretive in the sense that they do not wish to associate with the law, but I don't think that they're a secret society to the community.

As a result, he argued, young people in Craigmillar are more familiar with the nature of different drugs, their effects and their availability:

I am quite sure that our pupils know about the names of drugs, I think they know where to get them, I think they know who is selling them . . . I think they know costs. But it's one of those areas where they are also aware of the dangers. For the middle class child it can be a thrill, it can be an attractive risk, it can be something to try out, whereas for our kids, what they see is the horror of drugs, they *see* the needles, they *see* the drug addicts, they *see* the person dying of Hepatitis B.

It's what the children see around them - not a romantic image. When we talk to them in the school, they can connect up what we're talking about with their personal experiences, and their personal experience. That's why the school would regard this as an area in which we actively attempt to intervene and to work with the children - and we would feel that we could actually win in that area, unlike other areas such as theft where we don't expect to win.

These views certainly confirm our own observations in interviews. In comparison with young people in Craigmillar, the young people in Corstorphine and Marchmont in particular were much less knowledgeable about different types of drugs and the manner of their use. Young people interviewed in the schools in Wester Hailes and Broughton, on the other hand, appeared more conversant with at least some aspects of drug use and their dangers. Thus, the apparently recent arrival of large quantities of LSD in the city was widely discussed by young people at both the Broughton and Wester Hailes schools. For example, a 12 year-old girl in Wester Hailes was concerned to pass on the following information to her friends:

There's a new thing with people trying, taking acid pills. Well what I've heard aboot them is that you're not meant to take them when you're depressed cos they can make you do things that you dinnae even ken that you are doing. Like jumpin off a bridge and all that.

Another 13 year-old girl from Broughton was keen to demonstrate her own familiarity with the 'language' of acid:

A: They're no like that. I can say that for them. They've got brains like. No way I could imagine any of them injecting theirsels. A lot of them take acid just now.

D: Is that smoked?

C: Yes. *(very confidently)*

A: No, it's acid. 'Trippin' it. A good trip. But a lot of them do take that, I can say that. Mergalyn. *(Presumably mescalin)*

B: It's just a wee bit of paper. It's no like glue at all.

D: What is it? I've heard of acid but I've never . . .

At the school in Marchmont, especially among the younger people, there was clearly less familiarity, although the fear of injecting drugs was equally widespread. The following extract is taken from a discussion with 12 year-old boys in Marchmont. Note that the discussion of glue-sniffing takes the form of a 'cautionary tale':

C: Well, lots of drugs are just the same. Some people, they pay lots of money for a drug that's called heroin or something but they don't pay as much for drugs that are less known.

A: Or something that doesn't give you as much of a hit or something. For a start I wouldn't have the nerve to inject myself. It's horrible.

D: There's this drug that like it's 10,000 times as powerful as heroin . . . it's like this white stuff that you put on the end of a needle and it's really dangerous.

JW: *And what about glue-sniffing? Have you seen much of that?*

A: Glue-sniffing? I've never seen anyone doing in my life!

B: I've heard about people doing it. Like down town, in these toilets, there was a guy sniffing glue. And like nobody could find him and then an old man went into the toilets and it was locked and he went and told the man and the man came and opened it and this body just sort of fell out. And the glue went all over the ground. It was pretty disgusting.

A: One of my pals says he knew someone that tried to sniff glue and he got glucose drops!

106

Among the older boys at the school in Marchmont the distinction between hard and soft drugs appeared to be well known, as too were the dangers of AIDS and needle sharing. However, when asked which drugs in particular were hard and which soft, there was much less certainty. One boy, for example, described marijuana as a hard drug and 'hash' as a soft drug: 'There's some drugs you really get addicted to and you can't stop, like cocaine, marijuana and all these, the more purified stuff, but like hash and stuff it's easier to stop and your body won't have so many side-effects.' Similarly, as we saw above, the young girl from Broughton describes acid as 'mergalyn' and, despite her anxiety to appear knowledgeable before her friends, like them she was clearly unsure of what it was she had been taking 'just on Friday nights like.'

Thus, by second or third year, in all four areas, it was clearly believed that some drugs - 'hash' especially - were 'OK' while others were not so - especially those which are injected. Alongside the powerful images of the national advertising campaigns, which have emphasised that *all* drugs are bad, there thus appears a less informed set of ideas, which has clearly dissociated 'soft drugs' from 'hard drugs'. Official warnings are thus defused and subverted by an alternative set of subterranean beliefs, which fail to provide any detailed knowledge of what these hard drugs are and what effects they have. Thus, with the possible exception of Wester Hailes, few of those we interviewed were aware that heroin could be taken by means other than by injection. Indeed, there is a real possibility that some young people discriminate between hard and soft drugs simply by the mode of consumption - 'you inject hard drugs'.

In Wester Hailes especially, the experience of drugs and drug use is greater and much more threatening. This is especially so for the girls, who frequently expressed alarm at be approached by 'junkies' because of their unpredictable behaviour. The following discussion with a group of 15 year-old girls from Wester Hailes is worth citing at some length:

CS: *Is there much drug taking in Wester Hailes?*
A: Aye. *(all agree)* Everything.
B: Acid, hash anything they can get their hands on.
C: Valium.
CS: *Do any of you take drugs?*
B: Nuh.
C: Jist maybe a couple of puffs oot a joint.
CS: *What do you think about people who take drugs?*
A: I think it's no their fault cos they've nothin else tae dae.
C: I think it's alright if you have it once in a while. No if you're addicted to it then that's your fault.
CS: *Do you think that there is a difference between taking different kinds of drugs?*

107

All: Aye.
A: Like heroin and that.
C: If you smoke hash. It's no that bad but heroin and that ...
D: Hard drugs I wouldnae. There's a lot of difference.
CS: *Are there many folk your age that take hard drugs?*
A: Yeah. *(All agree)*
D: They take drugs but no hard drugs.
CS: *What about glue?*
All: Nuh.
A: I dinnae like that.
C: It gies you the creeps.
D: They're horrible.
A: They dinnae ken what they're doin so you dinnae trust bein with them. *(All agree)*
A: Nuh. I wouldnae *(take glue)* or hairspray or anything. I wouldnae touch that never. I wouldnae trust that, ken what I mean?
B: There's stuff you can trust and ken that you'll be alright but no with that.
A: I dinnae like all these junkies. You see junkies walking aboot the centre, jist a total mess. I dinnae think that's right, that's jist puttin an influence on people like us cos we're the next generation up.
B: Well they're kind of influencin us, teenagers. They're encouragin you.
A: If they're takin drugs and they say its barrie and that you think I want to try some it'll be good.
C: Aye but ye dinnae see older folk goin aboot the street sayin that you should take drugs its barrie, it's mair people of our age. Well you cannae say they're influencin us.
B: Aye but they're no daein. *(injecting)*
A: If they're goin tae dae it they should dae it in . . .
B: They could at least go into a toilet and dae it.
All: Aye.
A: They dae it in front of bairns and everything.
C: Aye people like that are jist idiots.

Such views are common among the young people of Wester Hailes. Their knowledge is direct and immediate. Their experience is one of horror and anger mixed with sympathy. As the headteacher said of Craigmillar, so for the young people of Wester Hailes drugs are neither romantic, nor something for which you have to search. In the following extract, from a conversation with girls of the same age from Broughton, we obtain a very different picture:

CS: *What about drugs, are there many drugs about?*
A: Hash. That's all you hear about.
B: I don't think serious drugs.
A: And acid.
C: Is there? I didn't know about that.
CS: *Is that folk your age or older?*
A: Hash? All ages.
CS: *Is it easy to get hold of then?*
D: I don't really know.
B: I don't know where to get it but I know people who know where to get it.
A: I know where to get it.
B: You know where you could ask.
CS: *Is there anyone trying to force drugs on you?*
A: No. It's not like that. You have to ask for it or go and find the person that knows where to get it. You have to go and find it yourself.
B: Well the drug dealers, it's a real con because they always raise the prices.
C: Give you coffee instead of hash.

The findings on drug abuse are not easy to interpret. Drug use is clearly widespread, especially among third and fourth years. For the young people in Wester Hailes, as for those we interviewed in Craigmillar, the meaning of drug abuse is very different from elsewhere in the city. In Wester Hailes and Craigmillar there is little if any romanticisation. To a much greater extent their immediate experience has taught them the difference between various types of drugs and the consequences of their use. For the girls in Corstorphine 'just buzzin gas' is 'OK', for young people in Wester Hailes using hair spray is out of order. For the young people in Broughton and Marchmont drugs are bought at a distance - through the same grapevine, presumably, which tells them soft drugs are harmless without saying which drugs are which.

Two general conclusions might be drawn. First, the apparent success of the local campaigns in Craigmillar requires careful evaluation. Has the success been maintained? If so on what basis can such initiatives be introduced elsewhere? In Wester Hailes, it would seem, there exists a similar cultural awareness and similar experiences of drug use as there were at the time we undertook the pilot at Craigmillar yet drug use appears to be more extensive. Can the lessons of Craigmillar be transferred? Are conditions different in Wester Hailes? How is it that local programmes (assuming there have been some) have not had the same purchase? All these questions need to be addressed as a matter of urgency.

Secondly, we might wish to question the impact of the national 'Choose Life' advertising campaign. While it is undoubtedly the case that the young people find the images frightening and the content serious, it also appears that their impact is in part defused and diluted by their own experience and half-knowledge of 'soft drugs'. This is not the place to consider the arguments about the legalisation of cannabis (a word, incidentally, which we never heard used among young people themselves). However, we would point out that, with the apparently wide availability and use of both marijuana and LSD among young people, advertising campaigns which fail to distinguish between different kinds of drugs and different forms of drug-taking run the severe risk of at best leading to confusion and at worst of becoming discredited.

We hesitate, on the basis of these findings alone, to suggest that young people should be instructed or taught in school how to recognise different types of drugs and to discriminate between them. We should reiterate the point that this research was not intended to look at this specific problem in any depth. However, if we are correct in this analysis, and if our data on use and availability stand up to the further research that we believe must be undertaken, then the issue of drugs education must be placed squarely back on the agenda.

'Serious' property crimes

In this section we look more closely at the findings on serious property crime - namely, housebreaking, shopbreaking and car theft. However, we should note that despite the size of our sample, the absolute numbers of young people committing such offences is small and we are limited in what can be said from the statistics. Thus, only 3% of young people at Corstorphine reported committing 'serious' property crimes although in other areas the rates were higher - Broughton 9%, Marchmont 6% rising to 11% in Wester Hailes. Nonetheless, before looking in any more detail at these findings and to keep them in perspective, we should note that even in Wester Hailes, the area with the highest incidence of offending, 89% of the young people surveyed had committed *none* of the offences included in this category. We should also stress that the figures on housebreaking and shopbreaking include attempts.

When we look at the incidence of serious property crime committed by boys rather than girls, differences between areas are much sharper. The number of boys at Corstorphine, who had committed one or more of these offences during the past nine months (5%), was almost 10% lower than Wester Hailes (15%) and Broughton (14%). In comparison, the rate among boys at Marchmont (10%) was again higher than in Corstorphine although not quite as high as in the other two areas.

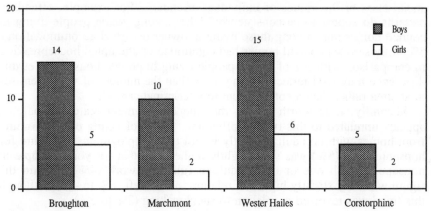

Figure 4.8
Young people committing 'serious' property crime by area and gender (%)

The figures for boys are sufficiently large to allow analysis of the incidence of different offence types among boys in the different areas. When this is done, we find the contrast between Wester Hailes, Broughton and Marchmont less pronounced, though the rates in Corstorphine are substantially much lower.

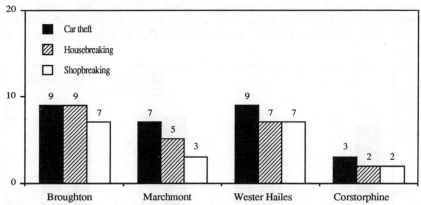

Figure 4.9
Boys committing 'serious' property crime by area (%)

Further interpretation of these findings would be unwise on the basis of the present research alone. However, two points from the interviews should be borne in mind. First, the differences between areas are probably better understood in terms of environmental differences rather than in terms of social class or the values of individual offenders. For example, offending patterns do appear to be consistently higher among young people living in council homes than among those living in owner occupied accommodation - 5% of those from council homes had committed or attempted housebreaking in comparison with 3% of young people living in private housing. Yet this difference may well reflect nothing more than the number of void premises in an area rather than a commitment to a 'criminal career'.

Secondly, it is worth noting that the employment status of parents appears unrelated to this type of offending. Thus, of young people coming from homes with no adult presently in full time employment, the figure for housebreaking (5%) was very slightly higher than that for young people in households with one or more adult in full time work (4%). Again the figure was very slightly higher in relation to car theft (6% to 4%), although this trend was reversed in relation to shopbreaking (2% to 3%).

'Less serious' offences

As we saw earlier, some two-thirds of the sample (66%) had committed at least one of the following: rowdiness in the street (48%); fighting in the street (43%); shoplifting (35%); property vandalism (30%) and car vandalism (14%). Thus, it should be stressed that such offending is not restricted to particular 'delinquent subcultures', nor is it concentrated among young people from particular social backgrounds. The simple fact is that *most* young people commit such offences, though, as we shall see later, they do so relatively infrequently. Thus, although we found some differences between offending rates among young people from different areas, more significant is the relatively high rate of offending across *all* areas.

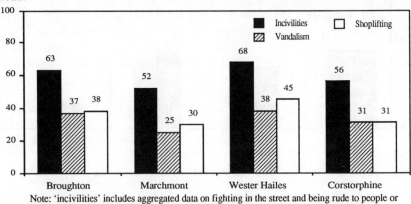

Note: 'incivilities' includes aggregated data on fighting in the street and being rude to people or rowdy in the street; 'vandalism' includes both property vandalism and car vandalism.

Figure 4.10
Young people committing 'less serious' offences by area (%)

As the following graph shows, gender differences in relation to petty offending are still pronounced but not as much as with the more serious offences analysed earlier. Thus boys are about twice as likely to fight and vandalise and break into cars as girls, but only marginally more likely to commit other forms of vandalism, to shoplift or to be rowdy or rude to people in the street.

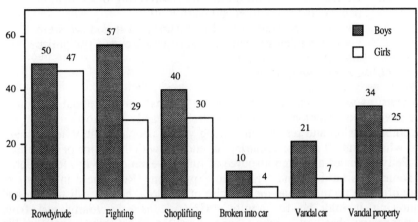

Figure 4.11
Young people committing 'less serious' offences by gender (%)

The widespread involvement of young people in petty offences raises a number of difficult questions of policy. First, for example, it would seem from the findings that problems such as vandalism can only be fully appreciated in the *aggregate* - that is, in terms of the *cumulative* effect of the relatively infrequent actions of a large numbers of young people. In such circumstances, it is difficult to penalise the individual as demanded by the law. Thus, looked at from the point of view of the *individual* offender, his or her acts will often appear trivial and inconsequential and certainly not meriting criminal charges. Alternatively, looked at from local residents' point of view, individual pieces of graffiti, for example, soon add up to a real *social* problem, with significant implications for policing and other local authority services:

CS: *What about vandalism, why do people do that?*
A: Cos they've got nothin else tae dae.
B: It's no only that is it? Cos if you're standin in a stairway and you've got a marker in you hand you jist write.
C: You jist colour in or something, you dinnae really think of it being bad or something.
B: Remember that stair we used to stand in it was covered.

113

A: That was the same stair next to this wifey's stair. She comes oot chasing us with frying pans and everything. She come oot swearin at us and everything and she had a fight with a wee lassie. She had a fight with the wee lassie, she was batterin the wee lassie. She was pullin her hair and everything. That was the wifey, but she's mad.

B: Ken we were writin on her stair with a big black marker pen we had to go doon and wash it off.

A: And her stair that had all oor names on it and we were goin to get charged before it got painted over. The police and all that were comin.

(13 year-old boys, Broughton)

Thus, as we saw earlier in relation to 'youths' hanging about in groups, the anger and irritation caused to adults can easily lead to confrontation, incomprehension and resentment among young people - 'the wifey's mad'; and what starts off as 'jist colouring in' ends up with the police being called.

Petty offences are often a source of fun and even creativity, for which it is sometimes hard to find legitimate expression. Rowdiness in the street may often be no more than the exercise of freedom, however disturbing and annoying it may be for adults. Graffiti, as one young girl from Corstorphine observed, can be a form of art: 'Maybe if they're interested in street art you could put up walls for it as an exhibition but vandalism like "somebody is a something", I don't think that's right. But pictures of dragons and things are brilliant, I like them.'

As we saw in relation to low level of drug use in Craigmillar, certain forms of 'expressive deviance', which are often manifested in particular cultural styles and practices, would appear to be open to challenge and prevention. Other offences, for example shoplifting and theft from cars, are of a very different quality and less readily open to change. For example, from this study and from other research we have undertaken, it is clear that in some areas of the city, organised shoplifting and the circulation of stolen goods play a major part in the local economy. A headteacher at a school in one of Edinburgh's peripheral estates explained how this could impinge upon his pupils:

If you go back thirty or forty years in this area there were a lot of very ragged children. Now you won't see any children who are ragged in this school. You'll see children who have very, very good leather jackets and wearing designer sweatshirts. But they did not buy that leather jacket from the shop, and there's no doubt that there is a value which says, 'Look, I'm entitled to be as well dressed as anybody else - if that means that I have to accept that either I shoplift myself, or I buy it for a third of the cost from somebody that I know shoplifted it, ok.'

114

So, what are you going to do? You're going to be poor and honest in a sense if you don't steal, and therefore visibly ragged when you walk down the street. Or are you going to accept another set of values. So there are value systems that are going to come through from the community. Indeed there's a parent in the school who has said to me, 'We don't associate with the shoplifting and I'm afraid my son feels a bit deprived, because he doesn't have the smart Benetton sweatshirts.'

In relation to such offences, it is difficult to feel any optimism in terms of crime reduction, as they are, without doubt, rooted in economic inequality and social divisions. Indeed, one of the very noticeable qualities of the interviews we carried out among young people from poorer areas of the city was the very practical awareness of poverty and social injustice they displayed in comparison with young people from other more affluent homes:

CS: *Do you think that there is any difference between stealing from a rich person and stealing from a poor person?*
A: Aye.
B: Rich persons got more.
C: It would be totally sneaky to steal from a poor person cos they can't afford anything.
B: The rich person wouldnae notice.
C: I think everybody should steal from rich people cos they've got to pay the same poll tax as us.
A: People like judges and that should pay more.
C: There shouldnae be a poll tax at all.
B: I know there shouldnae be any. We put a tent up and said 'No more poll tax.' The tent's still up.
(13 year-old boys, Wester Hailes)

CS: *What do you think a rich person is and a poor person is?*
A: A rich person is a total and utter snob.
B: Dead proud and that.
A: Think they're dead big, which they're not.
C: Its just like the difference between a state school and a private school. There's no difference it's just they've got more money.
CS: *If someone stole some food when they were hungry, do you think that they should get punished for that?*
C: If they were poor like? No. *(All agree)*
A: If they were homeless or something they should just steal it.

115

B: I feel sorry for the homeless.
A: It's Thatcher's fault though.
B: I ken.
A: Folk out on the streets and that, living in graveyards and that.
C: They should have places you can go to stay.
B: They should get some sort of allowance.
A: And the rent for hooses should be lower cos if they can afford to rent a hoose then they cannae afford to buy food as well.
B: Too many bills to pay. Family of five, £52 a week or something like that for food and bills and clothes.

(14 year-old boys, Wester Hailes)

The social background to offending

The extracts with which we ended the last section lead us naturally to look at the socio-economic characteristics and the social background of offenders. However, the wide distribution of petty offending across areas and gender, should immediately caution against any gross claims that offences can be attributed to an identifiable minority of young people coming from poorer areas of the city, such as Wester Hailes. Indeed, socio-economic class seems at best only contingently related to offending. For example, the occupational status of adult members of their household appears to have little or no bearing upon petty offending by young people.

From the following table it can be seen that offenders and non-offenders are equally likely to come from households where there is no adult in employment. For example, in relation to car vandalism we find that 48% of offenders come from households with two or more adults in full-time employment, 46% from households with one adult in full-time employment and 6% with none. When we look at the equivalent data for non-offenders, we find almost identical figures - namely, 49%, 44% and 7%. As can be seen from Table 4.3, this pattern is consistently repeated for other forms of vandalism, shoplifting and theft from cars as well as public disorderliness and other incivilities.

Table 4.3
Offenders/non-offenders by number of adults
in household in full time employment (%)

	Offender	Non-offender
Rowdiness in street		
None in full time work	7	7
One adult in full time work	40	48
Two or more adults in work	53	45
Fighting in street		
None in full time work	7	6
One adult in full time work	44	45
Two or more adults in work	49	49
Property vandalism		
None in full time work	7	7
One adult in full time work	41	46
Two or more adults in work	52	48
Vehicle vandalism		
None in full time work	6	7
One adult in full time work	46	44
Two or more adults in work	48	49
Shoplifting		
None in full time work	8	6
One adult in full time work	42	46
Two or more adults in work	50	48
Theft from cars		
None in full time work	6	7
One adult in full time work	54	44
Two or more adults in work	39	50

The analysis of the relationship between unemployment and petty offending can, however, be taken further. First, it has been suggested that a better index of the relation between offending and unemployment is the young person's evaluation of his or her own future employment prospects, rather than the employment status of their parents or adult members of their household. Again, however, we find no difference in patterns of offending among those who think it 'very' or 'fairly' likely that they will find a job when they leave school and those who think it 'not very' likely or 'very' unlikely.

Secondly, it has been widely argued that lack of attachment to the work ethic is a significant determinant of offending. If this is so, we would expect to find that offenders would worry considerably less about finding work on leaving school than non-offenders, who in turn would worry more than the offenders. Again, as can be seen from the table below, there is no evidence to support this hypothesis. Indeed, with the one exception of theft from cars where the findings go in the opposite direction from that expected, the level of anxiety expressed by offenders and non-offenders alike are extraordinarily similar.

Table 4.4
Worry about finding employment:
offenders and non-offenders (%)

	Worry a lot	Not much	Not at all
Rowdiness in street			
Non-offender	33	52	14
Offender	36	51	14
Fighting in street			
Non-offender	32	55	14
Offender	38	48	15
Property vandalism			
Non-offender	34	50	16
Offender	36	54	10
Vehicle vandalism			
Non-offender	35	51	14
Offender	33	54	13
Shoplifting			
Non-offender	34	52	14
Offender	35	51	14
Theft from cars			
Non-offender	34	52	14
Offender	44	42	14

From the analysis so far, we have seen that differences in offending cannot be explained simply in terms of the employment status of parents, young people's perception of their future job prospects or 'attachment to the work ethic.' An alternative explanation, frequently put forward in the popular press and elsewhere, lays emphasis on the lack of parental supervision and the amount of time young people (again usually working class young people) spend 'hanging about on the streets'. This view was reflected in the findings of the Edinburgh Crime Survey in which it was found that for many residents the number of teenagers hanging about the streets was perceived to be of general concern, as was the lack of facilities for young people in their area (Anderson *et al.*, 1990:9-13).

As we shall see, 57% of young people surveyed told us that they spend either 'a lot' or 'quite a lot' of their time simply 'messing about or hanging around' near home. It is perhaps surprising, therefore, that 80% of boys said there was either enough to do in the area (31%) or that they were only 'a bit' bored (49%). Girls were less satisfied, however - only 19% thought there was enough to do and 55% described themselves as 'a bit' bored.

Overall, 23% of young people described themselves as very bored in their area. However, differences were apparent between areas. Thus 32% of young people in Wester Hailes described themselves as 'very' bored as did 25% of those in Corstorphine in contrast with 18% in Broughton and only 16% in Marchmont. This suggests that proximity to the city centre may be a significant variable in Broughton and Marchmont.

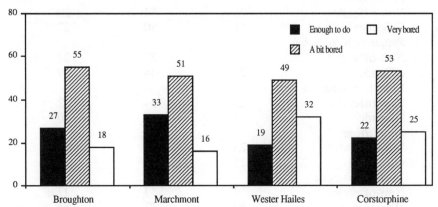

Figure 4.12
Young people's evaluation of the area in which they live (%)

It would be very convenient if, at this point, we could show a simple correlation between boredom and offending. Unfortunately, we cannot. Indeed, it is tempting to say that once again there is no direct relation between the two. Thus, for example, of those who had vandalised cars during the previous nine months, 28% say there is enough to do in their area, as did 25% of those who had not. Similarly, of those who had vandalised property, 23% of offenders say there is enough to do in comparison with 27% of non-offenders.

Nonetheless, although the relationship is by no means a strong one, there is a tendency for offending to increase with the level of boredom, as the next table shows. However, as we shall see, the relationship between offending and boredom is by no means straightforward.

119

Table 4.5
Evaluation of area by offenders/non-offenders (%)

	Enough to do	A bit bored	Very bored
Rowdiness in street			
Non-offender	27	54	19
Offender	23	50	27
Fighting in street			
Non-offender	26	54	20
Offender	23.	50	27
Property vandalism			
Non-offender	26	54	21
Offender	23	48	29
Vehicle vandalism			
Non-offender	25	54	22
Offender	28	42	30
Shoplifting			
Non-offender	25	52	23
Offender	25	52	23
Theft from cars			
Non-offender	24	53	22
Offender	30	37	33

Before progressing further with the analysis, we should perhaps pause if only to avoid the jump in logic which commonly occurs at this point. For, as we shall now see, too often we tend to fall back on the familiar images of bored and disconsolate teenagers hanging about street corners. In fact, for many young people, hanging about with friends and just 'messing about' is one of the more enjoyable features of their lives. However much of a problem this may pose for adults - whether as local residents, social workers or the police - for young people, it is (or rather, can be) fun.

From the graph below, we can see that a very substantial proportion of the young people surveyed (57%) spent either 'a lot' or 'quite a lot' of time 'hanging about or messing around' near home. Indeed, in Wester Hailes, this rises to over two-thirds of those interviewed in contrast to those at Marchmont for whom the figure falls to below half. While in part these findings may relate to the availability of desirable alternatives, it is also important to bear in mind how much enjoyment young people derive simply from being out and about on the streets with their friends - despite the many problems of victimisation we outlined earlier. Thus, when we asked young people who hang around 'a lot' how much they enjoy it, 84% described it as either 'really good' (48%) or 'quite good' (36%) while only 3% said it was 'really boring'.

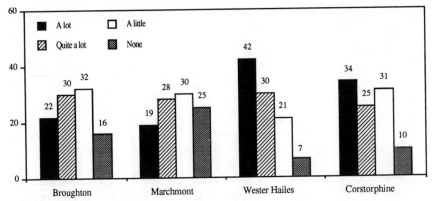

Figure 4.13
Amount of time spent 'hanging around' or 'messing about' by area (%)

Furthermore, the results tabulated below reinforce the view that hanging around the streets is an option that young people pursue because they enjoy it. Thus, the more boring they find it, not surprisingly, the less they do it.

Table 4.6
Amount of time spent 'hanging around or messing about' by how much enjoyed (%)

	Really good	Quite good	A bit boring	Really boring
A lot	48	36	13	3
Quite a lot	11	58	27	4
A little	3	39	44	13

This poses various difficulties from the point of view of policy making. First, as we have already noted, throughout the city the number of young people hanging around the streets is regarded as a problem by many residents. Secondly, as we have seen, the level of victimisation of young people in public places is considerable and must be of concern. Third, however, it appears that part of the entertainment derived from hanging about the streets can be put down to petty offending itself. Thus the following graph shows that offenders are considerably more likely to rate such activity as 'really good' than are non-offenders.

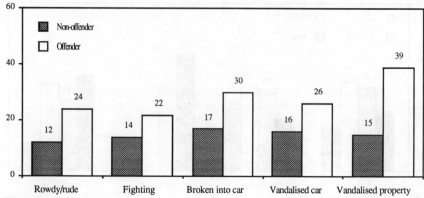

Figure 4.14
Young people rating 'hanging about' as 'really good': offenders and non-offenders (%)

Conclusion: learning the hard way

While it is important to recognise the real damage that can be done both by and to young people by crime, it is equally important to remember that crime can be fun for the young. In addition, it is important to recognise that rule-breaking is central to the process of learning the formal and informal rules of social life. Thus, the recognition of the critical role of children's games in learning rules and the acquisition of social norms has remained a central insight of educational and child psychology since the early work of Jean Piaget (1983). Strangely, however, criminologists and sociologists have shied away from the idea, forgetting that many if not most of the petty offences committed by young people are committed as part of a continuing game with adult authority, through which the formal and informal rules which constitute the world of the adult are discovered and assimilated by the child.

Thus earlier descriptive accounts, in which 'being chased by the police, shooting dice and skipping school was fun', have largely disappeared from the literature (cf. Bordua, 1961). In their place, we have a sequence of general theories in which delinquents are propelled into crime by forces beyond their comprehension or control and presented with an image of youth as disenchanted, alienated and above all bored. Indeed there are numerous theories which emphasise a full range of social, biological or psychological/medical pathologies, and all of which deny the child's capacity to think and act 'normally'.

Conversely, other theorists emphasise the *social* conditions which promote crime - stressing, for example, the disjuncture between legitimate expectations and economic opportunities and the social injustice of a world in which the child is found guilty at birth and predestined to a life of crime (Cohen, 1955; Cloward and Ohlin, 1960). Alternatively, other accounts rest more upon the *political* context of crime, emphasising the role of the courts, the police, the popular press etc. as the 'definers of deviance'. The 'delinquent' is thus the product of being singled out and 'labelled' by the powerful world of adult institutions and ideologies (Schur, 1973).

Certainly, there are moments when theories which emphasise the external conditions which shape and influence the child can usefully be brought into play. Economic crime, such as the organised shoplifting referred to earlier, can only be fully understood in terms of poverty and economic deprivation. Indeed, such work is essential if we are to understand the total process through which young people come into contact with and learn about crime and the criminal justice system. However, to assert that delinquency is exclusively the product of forces external to the child is once again to deny the autonomy of the child and to reproduce the refrain that the adult world knows best.

Thus, by denying the element of choice and creativity (present in the idea of play), such theories tend to reinforce popular images of the 'mindless' hooligan and to reproduce the contemporary obsession with the child as delinquent. Further, by focusing on only one dimension of the problem, they distort if not ignore the complex relations between the adult world, its rules and their enforcement and the young person's world, in which crime - whether experienced as victim, witness or offender - is a bewildering and contradictory phenomenon, sometimes frightening and sometimes fun but rarely predictable or comprehensible.

There is, however, a very different approach adopted by some, more radical criminologists, in which the world of the young person is the world of the youthful rebel. Thus youthful offending and, more widely, youth subcultures have been described in terms of 'ritualised resistance' - a form of rebelliousness, expressing (sometimes unwittingly) the rejection of an economic and social world which is systematically loaded against them (Hall and Jefferson, 1976). We have some sympathy with this approach as it abandons the wholesale criticisms which have been launched at young people and places the construction of 'the youth question' in a political context which would give a legitimate voice to the young.

This does not mean, however, that research should align itself uncritically with the views and attitudes of 'the underdog' (cf. Becker, 1970). As we have argued throughout this report, many of the strategies young people adopt to deal with crime can themselves be damaging and disruptive to their own lives as well as others. Nor should we romanticise or over-extend the idea of resistance or rebellion. As we have already suggested, many if not most responses young people make to crime are defensive and, as we have seen, young people are typified by their conventional rather than oppositional values.

This is not to say, however, that responsibility for petty or even more serious offending can be reduced, simplistically, to the rational choice of the individual. As we pointed out in the Introduction, young people have a very different way of conceptualising and perceiving the world and the social relations which compose it. The interviews we carried out provided many examples of this, particularly with the younger children. For instance, when asked to describe the difference between shoplifting and housebreaking, young people would immediately recognise that stealing personal possessions out of someone's house was wrong. Shoplifting, however, was distinctly more difficult to comprehend - if the goods have yet to be bought, who do they belong to? In the following extract, we see a 12 year-old girl from Craigmillar struggling to grasp a central concept of the criminal law - private property - and getting it wrong:

> Breaking into a poor person's hoose? I mean that's a sin. You cannae dae that. But stealing frae a shop . . . that's different. It all belongs the coonstil, ken?

Furthermore, while self-evident to the adult, the conditions under which 'rational choices' are made are circumscribed by factors other than the individual - for example, by one's class, ethnicity or gender. This will often prove problematic for young people. As cynical adults we can understand the way in which student 'pranks' are excused as 'high spirits', why male violence on a rugby pitch is perceived as a game, and why DSS fraud is prosecuted when tax evasion is not; a young person, however, asks 'Why is it that the same rules don't seem to apply?' Rather than confront a world in which choices would have predictable outcomes, to the child the adult world appears at best inconsistent, at worst duplicitous.

Young people at the age with which we are concerned spend a lot of their time learning when and which formal and informal social rules do and do not apply. For example, one boy of 15 knew what was going on when he was stopped by the police on his way back from cadets:

> Ken, I go tae cadets wi ma mates Fridays. The polis dinnae like people fae Niddrie up there but they never bother us cos we're in uniform. The other night we didnae have our uniforms cos we been cleaning the hall. They pulled us straight away. I just don't go there now cept fae cadets.
> *(15 year-old boy, Craigmillar)*

At 12, however, the application of different rules and their own response to rule-breaking by others can be a source of considerable confusion:

> Ken the teachers - they're always telling us aboot racism. One night I was going hame wi ma pal and there was this black boy

I ken. He's at oor school . . . I like him, ken. Anyway, there's these other girls across the road started shouting at him. 'Nigger' and that. So I went across an telt them an started fighting wi this wee girl that I kent an the polis came an took me hame. It wasnae fair, ken. The other lassie didnae get any trouble. I was only doin what the teachers said.

(12 year-old boy, Broughton)

As we have seen, such incidents - fighting in the street, messing about at bus stops - are typical of the mass of reported and unreported petty offences which young people experience as part of their everyday lives. Simply in terms of the extent and regularity of such offending among young people, the findings are interesting in themselves. Underlying these figures, however, there is the other story to be told. For while it is not our intention to *excuse* rule-breaking, we are concerned to *understand* it. And to understand rule *breaking*, we need to understand rule *learning*. Indeed, we suspect that the key to understanding much youthful offending lies in the simple and perhaps rather obvious point that, very often, it is only through breaking the formal and informal rules of the adult world that young people learn the boundaries of what is and is not permissible. In short, young people learn the hard way.

Let us take a relatively simple example to illustrate the complexity of this process. Sociologists of the police have documented the various informal rules that police officers employ in the selective enforcement of the criminal law (Manning, 1977; Reiner, 1978; Grimshaw and Jefferson, 1987). Although this may appear contrary to the idea of equality before the law and the formal rule of law itself, few adults would dispute that the exercise of discretion is an essential aspect of policing. For how else are the police to remain sensitive to the needs and demands of different situations? Pressure on resources, competing priorities at different times of the day or night, differences in problems in diverse areas can lead to a variety of practices and, consequently, to very different experiences for the police and of the police among sections of the population. Indeed, for the novice police officer, learning when to intervene and when not to, what to give high priority to and what to 'write off', when and who to listen to and who to ignore are fundamental lessons of the job.

For a young person, however, appreciation of the police officer's lot is not easy - it has to be learned. This is hard enough in relation to the written rules of law but even harder when the rules are varied informally according to an informal code often known only to officers themselves. It is harder still if the police fail to explain their action. In the next chapter, therefore, we shall consider the role of the police in this process whereby 'a bit of fun' can become 'big trouble'.

5 Young people and the police

Introduction

In this chapter we shall present the findings on young people's relations with the police. These findings will be presented and analysed in terms of young people's attitudes towards and their contact with the police, and the way in which this contact relates to their experiences as victims of crime as well as users of public places.

Our focus, however, shall be somewhat different from that which usually informs research in this area. Throughout this study, our wish has been to move away from a stereotypes of young people as 'hooligans' or 'delinquents' who present a constant problem *for* the police. Instead, we are concerned with taking seriously young people's perceptions of the police and looking at policing in terms of how young people experience it. This requires that we address ourselves to what young people want as recipients of a police service, and examine how this squares with their experience of the police.

One of the most striking and important findings to come out of the pilot study in Craigmillar was the deep ambivalence displayed by young people towards the police. By this we mean that the police are perceived by young people as a source both of protection and of control, and that this occasions very contradictory feelings and responses. Thus, from our interviews with young people in Craigmillar it seemed that while they clearly wanted more police on the street for protection, they also resented some of the practices they anticipated such increased policing would bring.

These feelings appeared to be rooted in, on the one hand, the high levels of victimisation they suffered; and on the other, in their actual experience of policing - in particular the high levels of adversary contact with the police they had experienced. Indeed, two-thirds of the young people we spoke to had come into some form of adversary contact with the police, ranging from being moved on to being arrested and taken to a police station. It should also be emphasised that these findings related only to the previous nine months and that it is probably fair to assume that, over a longer recall period, an even higher proportion would have experienced such contact.

It was also striking that this contact was not necessarily met with hostility by the young people concerned. For example, 59% thought that the last time they were questioned, the police officer had acted fairly. However, this percentage fell to 32% of those who had been stopped and searched. This suggested that far from being universally anti-police, young people in Craigmillar can and do discriminate between what they see as 'good' and 'bad' police practice and that their evaluation of police action varied according to the practice involved.

The pilot study also showed that young people's experience as victims of crime contributes to their ambivalence towards the police. Young people in Craigmillar wanted more policing for protection against some of the dangers that the streets hold. Thus, 66% told us they would 'feel safer if there were more police officers on patrol on foot' - a figure that rose to 77% for the girls, while falling slightly to 54% for the boys. Yet of the 77% of the girls who wanted more foot patrols, 59% felt that the police were unfair in their dealings with young people.

From these findings it seemed that young people in Craigmillar were confused about the police. They wanted more policing, while expressing concern about its consequences. They were perplexed as to why the police spent so much time responding to complaints made against them, yet failed to take their complaints seriously. Above all else, these perceptions seemed rooted in experiences which, we felt, warranted further exploration:

RK: Why would you like there to be more police about?
A: All the men, the weirdos.
B: You're always bein followed and that flashers.
A: I was in the lift at my aunties hoose with my wee sister. And this man got in and took doon his trousers. We screamed and screamed but we couldn't get out till we got down. Then we ran off but he didn't chase us or anything.
B: You're always frightened of getting jumped on ken.
RK: What do you mean 'getting jumped on'?
B: Gettin raped and that.
C: The alkies and the junkies. They come up to you saying things. They try to get into your claithes.
RK: So is that why you want more police?
All: Yeah.
A: Mind, you wouldnae want too many, eh? I mean, they'd be watching you all the time, catching you an that. It wouldnae be any fun if there was too many.

The pilot study, then, indicated quite clearly that young people's attitudes and perceptions of the police were far more complex than is commonly supposed. Very few young people seem to fit the anti-police stereotype into which they are so often cast by academics, journalists and policy-makers. Rather, they have a more contradictory attitude towards the police, born of their experiences *both* of crime and of the police. In this chapter we shall explore these contradictions and analyse their consequences.

General attitudes towards the police

The first part of the chapter presents the findings on young people's attitudes towards the police and their contact with them. With regard to the first of these issues, we asked young people about their views on police understanding of their problems; whether they felt the police treated young people fairly, and whether they had ever been pleased or displeased with the police.

Again, a polarised rather than a consistent picture emerges. Over the four areas, just under half (49%) thought that the police had a 'very' good (6%) or 'quite' good (43%) understanding of the problems young people face, while the remainder (52%) thought that they had either a 'quite' poor (32%) or 'very' poor (20%) understanding of their problems.

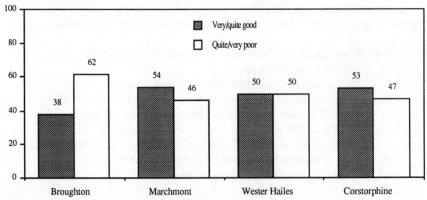

Figure 5.1
Police understanding of young people by area (%)

When broken up by area (see figure 5.1 above), again no consistent picture emerges, with young people at the schools in Marchmont and Corstorphine having a more favourable impression of the police. It is also worth noting that young people's evaluation of the police declines with age. Thus, 61% of 12 year-olds thought the police had a 'very' or 'quite' good understanding of their problems, a figure that drops to 41% for 15 year-olds. Differences were also apparent in terms of gender: 44% of boys thought the police understanding 'very' or 'quite' good while 54% of girls did so.

A similar picture emerges regarding young people's evaluation of whether the police treat young people fairly. Overall, 54% thought the police treated young people fairly, while 46% thought they were unfair. However, a more striking picture appears when the findings are broken down by age and area. Thus, 66% of 12 year-olds felt the police treated young people fairly, dropping to 47% of 15 year-olds, and as the following graph shows, a less favourable evaluation of the police is held by young people living in the Broughton area and Wester Hailes.

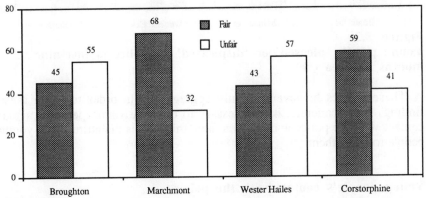

Figure 5.2
Perceptions of how fair the police are to young people by area (%)

A further indicator of both young people's contact with and evaluation of the police was obtained by asking whether they had been 'pleased' or 'displeased' by the police. In general terms, 31% had been pleased by a police action in the previous nine months, while 23% had been displeased. However, when broken down by area (see the graph below), these findings reveal that young people at the schools in Broughton and Wester Hailes have experienced more contact with the police, whether that contact be of a satisfactory or unsatisfactory nature. A similar pattern emerges with regard to gender, with boys more likely to be both 'pleased' by police action (33% compared to 28% of girls), and 'displeased' by police action (28% as against 17% of girls).

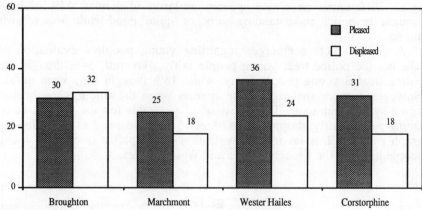

Figure 5.3
Young people 'pleased' or 'displeased' by police in last nine months by area (%)

These figures however are only aggregates. In order to make these findings more concrete, it is necessary to examine young people's actual contact with the police and examine how this effects the attitudes of young people towards them.

Young people's contact with the police

Police-initiated contact

In the pilot study in Craigmillar, we found that young people had considerable adversary contact with the police, far higher than comparable levels of contact for adults living in the same area (Kinsey, 1992). These findings prompted us to ask whether such figures were peculiar to the policing of Craigmillar, or whether such levels of contact would be replicated in different areas of the city.

We therefore asked whether young people had - 'since the beginning of the last summer holidays' - been 'moved on or told off', 'questioned about crime', 'arrested or detained' or 'stopped and searched' by a police officer. Across all four areas, 44% had been moved on or told off; 25% had been questioned about a crime; 13% had been stopped and searched, and 10% had been arrested or detained in a police station. All in all, some 51% of the total sample had experienced some form of adversary contact with the police.

The first thing to notice about these results are the stark differences that exist between them and the comparable figures for the adult population. Data from the Edinburgh Crime Survey (Kinsey, 1992) show that only 2%

130

of respondents in central Edinburgh had been stopped and searched by the police; 1% of those in Corstorphine and 2% of those living in Craigmillar. The highest comparable figure related to men aged 16-30, 7% of whom had been stopped and searched. A similar picture emerges in relation to questioning, with only 5% of adults in central Edinburgh; 2% in Corstorphine and 6% in Craigmillar having been stopped and questioned by the police. Again, the highest comparable group were males aged 16-30, 15% of whom had been questioned by the police. In the graph below, these figures are broken down by age.

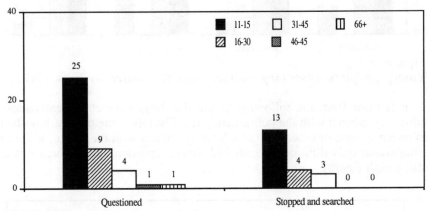

Figure 5.4
Adversary contact with the police by age - Edinburgh Crime Survey, 1990 (%)

This seems to indicate that considerable police attention in the city is focused on people under the age of 16 and we shall explore some of the possible reasons for - and consequences of - this below. First, we need to look at the results on young people in more detail.

It is apparent from the following graph that young people's contact with the police is higher - for all forms of police-initiated contact - in both Broughton and Wester Hailes. Thus, if we take adversary contact as a whole, 64% of those living in Wester Hailes, and 54% of those living in the Broughton area, had experienced some form of adversary contact with the police, while 46% of those in Corstorphine and 42% of those at the school in Marchmont had had similar contact. Despite these differences, it is evident that a substantial number of young people had come into adversary contact with the police, irrespective of where they lived.

131

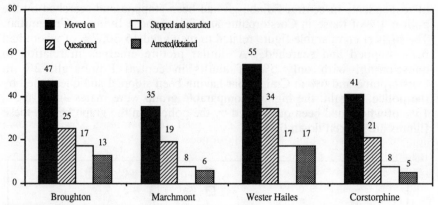

Figure 5.5

Young people's adversary contact with the police by area (%)

It is clear from the following graph, that boys have consistently more adversary contact with the police than girls. Overall, some 62% of boys had experienced one or other form of adversary contact with the police, while in comparison only 40% of the girls had similar experiences (although this is still a high figure).

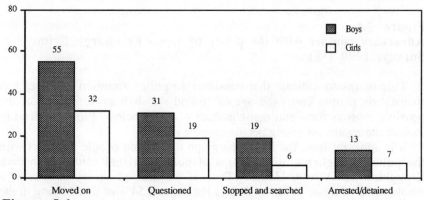

Figure 5.6

Young people's adversary contact with the police by gender (%)

This is likely to relate to a number of factors. First, it seems less likely that girls are stereotyped as 'trouble' in the same way as boys - either by the police or by adults in general. Consequently, they are likely to become the subject of police attention to a far lesser extent. Moreover, as we argued in Chapter 2, girls' 'violence' to one another takes on a physical form less often. Though we can only speculate on this point, it seems that girls more often employ techniques of 'shunning' and verbal abuse, rather than more

132

direct physical confrontation. In the present context, it seems that such 'violence' is both less visible and less likely to attract adult concern and reaction.

A more general observation can also be made. Irrespective of area or gender, the majority of adversary contact young people have with the police consists of being moved or told off. For some, though by no means all, such contact appears to be frequent. Of those that had come into contact with the police in this way, 46% had done so on three or more occasions. This compares with 29% of those arrested and detained, 26% of those stopped and searched and 18% of those questioned. We shall see below that this high level of contact is a consistent complaint of the young people against the police, and significantly colours their perception of policing. This issue can best be introduced by looking at young people's evaluation of their contact with the police.

Young people's evaluation of police contact

In order to gauge how young people evaluated their contact with the police they were asked whether, on the last occasion they had experienced adversary contact they thought the 'police officer had acted fairly.' In response, 45% said they thought the officer had acted fairly the last time they had been moved on; 60% the last time they were questioned about a crime; 38% the last time they were stopped and searched, and 41% the last time they were arrested or detained.

These figures hardly indicate the existence of a group of young people who are ardently anti-police. Indeed, at first sight they seem to show that a large number of young people generally concur with the police officer's conduct. However, the results also suggest that young people discriminate between what they see as 'good' and 'bad' policing. Thus, 60% thought the police officer fair in stopping and questioning them about crime - an encounter that is likely to be more consensual, especially where the young person concerned is not under suspicion. On the other hand, only 38% felt that the police were fair to stop and search them, an encounter which constitutes far more of a imposition on the young person involved.

This picture, however, needs qualifying in a number of ways. First, it is necessary to look at the effect of police officers giving a reason for their actions on young people's evaluation of their conduct. Secondly, it is essential to look at the effect of repeated adversary contact on young people's perceptions of the police.

We asked young people whether, the last time they had come into adversary contact with the police, they had been given a reason for the police action. Of those who had been moved on or told off, 58% were given a reason; 65% of those questioned were given a reason; 59% of those stopped and searched and 73% of those arrested or detained. These figures may, at first sight, seem quite high. But it ought to be remembered that police officers are under a legal obligation to give reasons if they stop and search or arrest and detain people. In this light, the fact that well over a quarter of the young people arrested or detained by the police were given no explanation, is, to say the least, worrying. Of course, it may well be the case that these people were given a reason, but that they either failed to understand it, or felt it to be inadequate. The important point, however, is that young people's views on the police are significantly coloured by their understanding of the police's action.

An important contributory factor in this regard may also lie in the comparatively low numbers of young people actually charged by the police following these incidents. Thus of those questioned, 15% were charged with an offence; of those stopped and searched - where at law the officer must have reasonable grounds to suspect an offence - the number charged was still only 24%. Indeed, even in the case of arrest and detention, less than half (43%) were charged with an offence.

The lack of formal charges or an explanation for the police officer's action has a serious effect on the impact of that action on the young people involved. As can be clearly seen from the table below, those young people who were not given a reason for the police officer's action were consistently more likely to perceive the encounter negatively. Though, in the case of stop and search and arrest the numbers are relatively small, and not statistically significant, the differences here are especially striking. It would seem, therefore, that the provision of an explanation is a major factor in determining how adversary encounters with the police are viewed by young people.

Table 5.1
Perceived fairness of police action
by whether given a reason (%)

	Given reason		Not given reason	
Police action	Fair	Unfair	Fair	Unfair
Moved on	57	43	27	73
Questioned	71	29	39	61
Stopped and searched	54	46	13	87
Arrested or detained	50	50	17	83

The second issue we have to consider concerns the effect of adversary contact on young people's general evaluation of the police. It is important to note, however, that adversary contact is not the only way that young people come into contact with the police. In recent years, the police have placed considerable emphasis on developing positive contact with young people through schools and youth clubs. In addition, police officers are encouraged to use their time on the streets to develop positive relations with young people. In determining the effect of contact with the police on young people's attitudes towards them, the level of social contact must be taken into account.

A rough indication of the degree of 'social contact' can be gauged from the table below. As can be seen, over half the young people in the sample had experienced some social contact on the street or at school during the previous nine months. However, contact of this nature appeared to be negligible in youth clubs and during other recreational activities. It is noticeable however, that over two-thirds (68%) of young people had experienced some form of 'social contact' with the police during the previous nine months, and that, in addition, 29% felt they knew a police officer well enough to stop and talk to in the street.

Table 5.2
Young people's 'social contact' with the police (%)

Met and talked to police officers . . .	Never	Once or twice	Three or more times
in the street	52	36	12
at school	59	33	7
at a youth club	90	9	1
during other recreation	78	17	5

The effect of such contact is more difficult to ascertain. Certainly, the qualitative data seems to indicate that, as well as discriminating between good and bad policing, young people distinguish between good and bad police officers:

There's one I knew, my pal, but he moved away . . . but he was alright.
(13 year-old boy, Broughton)

There's no enough of them around, no the kind of local policemen.
(12 year-old girl, Marchmont)

In a similar vein, one 12 year-old girl in Craigmillar told us (by name) about a local policeman she knew and liked, with whom she compared other officers very unfavourably. Upon further enquires it turned out that this particular constable had been transferred to another division some four years earlier, at which time the girl concerned would have been eight. It seems that good memories can last. However, as the table below suggests,

135

social contact with the police seems to have only a slight effect on young people's general perception of the police understanding of their problems.

Table 5.3
Social contact by evaluation of police understanding (%)

Social contact with the police	Very good	Quite good	Quite poor	Very poor
No	3	48	32	18
Yes	7	41	33	20

Furthermore, as we can see from the following table, adversary contact appears to have a more significant negative effect on young people's perceptions of the police.

Table 5.4
Adversary contact by evaluation of police understanding (%)

Adversary contact with the police	Very good	Quite good	Quite poor	Very poor
No	8	58	26	9
Yes	4	29	38	29

Similar results are found when we examine young people's perception of how fair the police are. The group of young people with the highest evaluation of the police, in this respect, were those who had experienced no adversary contact with them at all. Thus 76% of those who had experienced social contact but no adversary contact thought that the police, in their area, treated young people fairly. Furthermore, 70% of those young people who had no contact at all with the police were of the view that the police were fair in their dealings with young people. In very marked contrast, as few as 33% of those whose only experience was adversary contact thought that the police treated young people fairly.

These results are reinforced when one looks at the effects of repeated adversary contact on young people's perceptions of the police. Of the 51% of the sample who have had adversary contact with the police 40% had done so on one or two occasions, and 11% (n=92) on three or more occasions. It is clear from the table below that the more young people come into adversary contact with the police, the lower their perception of them becomes. Of those who had come into adversary contact with the police on three or more occasions, only 13% thought the police treated young people fairly. 60% of this group had also been displeased with the police during the previous nine months, compared with only 5% of those who had experienced no adversary contact during that period.

Table 5.5
Repeated adversary contact by evaluation of the police (%)

Adversary contact with the police	Very good	Quite good	Quite poor	Very poor
Never	8	58	26	9
Once or twice	5	32	39	24
Three or more times	1	19	31	50

This would seem to suggest that police contact perceived to be unjust has a far greater effect on young people's perceptions than the occasional positive contact in the street or the classroom. This relates to a point that we shall develop in more detail below. We suggested in Chapter 4 that, in part, young people's offending can be seen as part of a rule-learning process. In so far as this is the case then, given the levels of adversary contact shown by these findings, the police obviously play a pivotal role in this process. A vital aspect of young people 'learning the rules' about what is right and wrong, is drawn from their experience of how the police deal with them in a variety of situations. From these results and the interviews we carried out, it seems that young people perceive police officers to be unpredictable in the way they behave. While one may politely ask you to move along, another may order you to do so, giving no reason and leaving the young person concerned resentful and confused.

In trying to make sense of this unpredictability, young people are more likely to take heed of adversarial encounters than 'social' ones. For, only by learning the lessons of the former negotiations can young people best 'keep out of trouble' with the police. Seen in this light it should be no surprise that young people perceptions of the police are largely determined by their adversary experiences of them. Young people store up memories of unfair treatment at the hands of the police to a degree that has no equivalent in terms of their social contact (Matza, 1964). This becomes clearer if we look at young people's perceptions of the police in more depth.

137

Ambivalence towards the police: over-control and under-protection

Over-control: young people's perceptions of adversary contact

If we are to ascertain what young people want from the police service and evaluate the extent to which these demands square with their experiences, it is essential to grasp the relationship between young people, crime and policing in its entirety. An adequate analysis of young people's understanding of policing therefore requires reconsideration of the question of their victimisation; for it is only by looking at the whole range of contact young people have with crime, that we can begin to understand the meaning of policing to them.

We saw earlier that young people under the age of 16 are subject to far higher levels of police-initiated contact than those aged 16 and over. One possible explanation for these differences, is that the police come under pressure from the adult population to 'move on' groups of young people who adults perceive as a 'nuisance'. Indeed, police officers often claim that in moving on young people, they are merely responding to demands from local residents.

Comparative data from the Edinburgh Crime Survey (Anderson *et al.*, 1990) gives some indication that this is the case. For example, in Broughton, 48% of residents saw 'teenagers hanging about the streets' as either a 'big' problem (18%) or 'a bit' of a problem (30%), while in Craigmillar, 72% of respondents saw teenagers as a 'big' problem (39%) or 'a bit' of a problem' (33%). In interviews with young people it was apparent that many of them recognised that much police-initiated contact was in reality originated in the complaints of adults:

> I suppose a lot of old folk who live round here, I suppose they get scared if they see groups of folk around and call the police. They are alright about it but they dinnae really give you a good enough reason for moving you.
> *(14 year-old girl, Corstorphine)*

> Cos if there's a group of us and we're just wandering aboot or we're sittin in a stair or somethin, make a noise and the person comes oot and tells you to move or they'll phone the police, so you have tae move.
> *(14 year-old girl, Wester Hailes)*

> When your oot at night and if you make a noise or anything someone ends up phoning the police and you end up gettin told to move and it's jist . . .
> *(14 year-old girl, Wester Hailes)*

138

Indeed, many young people recognise that, for adults, such groups can be threatening:

> A:　You're walking along the road and you've got quite a lot of people, and somebody phoned the police cos they were worried something was going to go wrong. Whenever they see a big group of people they think, oh what's going on here, there's going to be trouble.
>
> SA:　*Do you think that's fair?*
>
> A:　I suppose . . . they're only making sure, but it's not really fair if you havenae done anything.
>
> *(12 year-old boy, Broughton)*

We suggested in Chapter 3 that 'hanging around' in groups is one of the strategies young people employ to ensure their own protection. The irony of this, as we have seen, is that many adults perceive such groups as threatening and resort to the police. The result is that one of young people's means of coping with crime merely brings them into further adversary contact with the police. This goes some of the way towards explaining why young people's appreciation of adult concern is coupled with bewilderment and resentment about its consequences for them.

A number of more general points arise from young people's interpretations of their adversary contact with the police. First, many of them thought that merely being on the streets in groups made them readily susceptible to police attention. This is combined with the feeling that they themselves were doing no harm, and they could see no understandable motive for the police action. This is compounded if police officers offer no adequate explanation.

This impression that the police's attention was unwarranted is exacerbated by the perception that the police do not take seriously their more serious problems of victimisation and safety. Thus, even when young people realised they were doing something wrong, they often considered their actions petty and trivial compared with the more serious things which happened to them, for which the police provide little or no protection. Both of these issues tie in with a more general one: namely, that their views and problems are not listened to, either by adults in general or the police in particular.

As a result, young people's perceptions of police behaviour centrally revolve around the idea that they are singled out for attention merely because they are young, in a group, and out in a public place:

> If you're on the streets and that and you're in a group and they drive past, they'll slow down and that. You're not doing anything and you'll get lifted.
>
> *(14 year-old girl, Corstorphine)*

If you're hanging aboot in a group and that just going to a youth club or something they stop you and say 'Move on please.'
(13 year-old boy, Broughton)

We were walking along and the police stopped their car, must have been about 10 o'clock - 'Alright boys where yous going?' 'Just been playing fitba' 'Yous knows you shouldn't be oot in big groups.' There was four of us, two little boys, two teenage boys!
(14 year-old boy, Wester Hailes)

In some cases, these views were coupled with a practical understanding of the daily realities of policework:

Some of them are so bored they would stop and hassle you if you're just standing around.
(14 year-old girl, Marchmont)

They just drive around, cos they're bored they just look for somebody to chase.
(13 year-old boy, Wester Hailes)

I suppose they get a bit bored and they think well we might as well have a bit of a laugh.
(14 year-old boy, Wester Hailes)

Many of these accounts of police contact and practice involve young people trying to come to terms with what they perceive to be the unpredictability and irrationality of much policework. They are attempts by young people to provide themselves with explanations for what they often think of as unjustified police action.

The following extract is taken from a series of interviews we conducted with police officers for the Safer Edinburgh Project (Kinsey, 1992). It is included here as it provides some insight into these issues from a police officer's point of view, and because it illustrates the ambiguities young people can experience:

We spend half our time chasing them *(young people)* about. I don't know if they treat it as a game, they never seem to fight with the police. You're just moving them on from one place to another. Well, they were hanging about Broughton Street and down that area and my inspector, he was quite good, he says 'Right, tonight we'll just lock em all up - do them for breach of the peace.' It solved the problem for the Broughton Street area because they just went somewhere else because they realised they'd just get locked up if they stayed there. If that was happening to them in every division where they congregate, they'd soon get the message.

In response to such actions, the rationalisations that young people employ are part of the process by which young people learn the 'rules' of policing as they are applied to them on the street - in other words, how they 'get the message'. Thus, for some young people police 'boredom' offers one reason (in the absence of the availability of others) why the police devote so much attention to them. Others account for police action simply in terms of 'stereotyping' - based on either age, the place you live, or how you look:

> Sometimes they dinnae do anything to help you. Everyone 15 or 16 is classed as a stereotype, all drinkin and rowdy vandalism.
> *(14 year-old girl, Corstorphine)*

> They think we do things and we're all wee criminals. Cos of the area.
> *(15 year-old boy, Wester Hailes)*

> A: And one o ma pals from school, we were at this garage and the police were goin aboot and she got lifted jist cos she was walking about, standin in the centre. She got lifted cos o that, they jist took her name. Well they took her name and we were given warnings and all that.
> CS: *What for?*
> A: Jist standin aboot, like bein in a crowd sort of thing. But I bet if she'd had a skirt on or something they wouldn't thought nothing of it.
> B: Aye, that's jist sort of . . .
> A: It's jist the way you look. If you look as though you're a troublemaker then . . .
> *(15 year-old girls, Wester Hailes)*

Indeed, such stereotypes of young people are often found among police officers themselves. In the following account, a police officer describes the tactics he employs when dealing with young people in the Southside:

> A: We need to get about them. To have more police on the streets and hassle them a wee bit. It possibly won't solve the problem, but they need to be aware that the police are there. They give everybody a hard time. So we select the areas where they congregate like the Southside. We make

them aware of our presence. We need to take a hard line view.

IL: *Under what circumstances do you move young people on?*
A: If they are causing a disturbance or shouting abuse, or if I recognise them as troublemakers, or if I thought they are going to cause trouble. If they are 'casuals' I move them on right away. They cause us and the public a lot of bother.

None of this is meant to suggest that young people are 'little angels' being harassed by unjust police practices. As we have seen from the chapters on both victimisation and offending, young people can and do cause a considerable amount of harm and annoyance, both to their peers and to adults. Indeed, some of the young people interviewed could readily understand the reasons for the police action:

> I've been chased by CID many a time, just like for minor things, like maybe smashing a windae or something. There used to be a big massive factory, was shut doon, right? When you walked past you usually just chucked a stane at the windae, all the windaes were smashed. The CID would see you right? They'd chase you for absolute miles. They take your name or take you doon the station.
> *(13 year-old boy, Wester Hailes)*

However, young people's perceptions of the police are more complex than mere resentment of the degree of police attention. The point of accounts like this one is they indicate the feeling among young people that they are constantly the subject of police attention for 'minor' things. Though many young people indulge in petty offending or mess around on the street with their friends, they themselves consider this behaviour relatively trivial and unimportant. For example, we saw in Chapter 4 that many young people commit acts of vandalism. But they do so infrequently and regard their actions as fairly insignificant.

This goes some way towards explaining why being moved on and warned by the police engenders so much bewilderment - even resentment - among young people. The issue for young people themselves is not so much that the police unfairly discriminate against them; but rather, that police priorities appear so askew when set against the more serious problems they experience in terms of victimisation. As the same 13 year-old boy so succinctly put it:

> They're wasting their time chasing you for a minor thing when they could be chasing someone else for a big thing.

Similar sentiments were echoed by a 15 year-old girl from the Broughton:

> About my area they *(local teenagers)* were doing something
> silly and they had the police and CID guys up, millions of them
> just for that one thing and there was bigger crimes than that
> about.

Under-protection: young people's perceptions of safety and police priorities.

This sense of perplexity at police behaviour brings us back to the
question of policing and young people's safety. As we saw in Chapter 2,
young people experience levels of victimisation far exceeding those of the
adult population. For them, the streets and other public places can be
dangerous and hostile. These factors mark young people out as a group
with a considerable degree of need for a police service. Thus, it is certainly
not the case that young people are unequivocally hostile towards the police.
This will be seen if we look more closely at young people's perception of
the police's role in their safety.

In the questionnaire, young people were asked if they would feel safer
with more police patrolling on foot and in cars. Overall, 55% said that they
would feel safer with more foot patrol officers and 49% said they would
feel safer with more car patrols. As the following graph shows, a majority
of both girls and boys would feel safer with more police (with the slight
exception of boys' perception of car patrols).

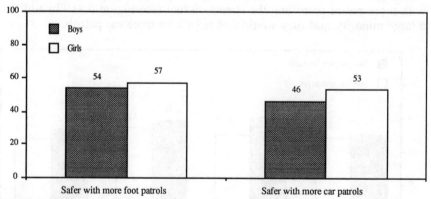

Figure 5.7
Perceptions of safety with more police patrols by gender (%)

These figures indicate the relationship between young people's anxieties
about crime and the demands they have regarding the provision of policing.
As we saw in Chapter 3, girls worry considerably more than boys about

their safety in public places. Indeed, it is those young people who worry most about crime that have the greatest wish for more police. For example, 70% of those who worry about being alone after dark wanted more police foot patrols, compared with only 46% of those who this did not concern. The relationship between young people's worries and the demand for more police can be seen in more detail in the table below. Thus, while 55% of those who worry 'a lot' about being attacked by strangers would feel safer with more foot patrols, only 40% of those who do not worry 'at all' about this would do so.

Table 5.6
Worry about crime by safer with more police (%)

| | Worries about crime | | | | | | | |
| | Attack by stranger | | Attack by person known | | Things being stolen | | Out alone at night | |
Safer with more police patrols on...	*Foot*	*Car*	*Foot*	*Car*	*Foot*	*Car*	*Foot*	*Car*
A lot	60	55	65	58	56	52	65	60
Not much	51	44	53	48	56	47	59	51
Not at all	45	40	47	42	46	43	44	40

Across the four areas, over half the sample said they would feel safer with more police patrolling the streets on foot (see Figure 5.8). In addition a large minority said they would feel safer with more car patrols.

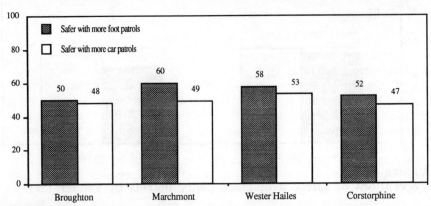

Figure 5.8
Young people who would feel safer with more police patrols by area (%)

144

The highest numbers holding these views can be found among young people at school in Marchmont and Wester Hailes. Young people in the former area, generally had the least contact and most favourable perceptions of the police of all the areas covered. It is no perhaps no surprise, therefore, that the provision of more police officers would make them feel safer.

However, the situation in Wester Hailes is more complex. Young people in this area have the highest levels of adversary contact with the police and a lowest evaluation of them of all the four areas. Nonetheless, a majority of them would feel safer with more police - both on the streets and in cars. Young people it seems are ambivalent in their attitudes towards the police: high levels of adversary contact and a low impression of the police, sits uneasily alongside a demand for more police.

From the table below it can be seen that the more adversary contact young people have had with the police, the less likely they are to see the risks of crime reduced by an increased police presence. It is interesting to note, however, that 29% of those who have experienced repeated adversary contact would still feel safer with more police officers patrolling the streets.

Table 5.7
Adversary contact with the police by
feeling safer with more police (%)

Adversary contact with the police	Safer with more foot patrols		Safer with more car patrols	
	Yes	No	Yes	No
Never	66	35	57	43
Once or twice	50	50	48	52
Three or more times	29	71	21	79

These considerations take us to the heart of the question of young people's ambivalence towards the police. To look at either adversary contact between young people and the police, or the police's role in young people's safety in isolation, is to miss the point. The important issue is the *relationship* between these two phenomena. When viewed in this context, it is no surprise that those who have had repeated adversary contact with the police are more wary of the effect of more policing on their safety. They fear that an increase in the provision of police officers will result in more policing *of* them, not more policing *for* them.

Young people's ambivalence towards the police is not, therefore, directed at the police *per se*, but rather at certain police practices and priorities. Young people's confusion at the extent and nature of police attention they receive thus occurs in the context of fears about their own safety and the perceived lack of police understanding of their problems. This has two aspects to it. First, it revolves around the fact the police waste so much time 'hassling' them when, in their view, there are more important matters at hand. To young people, it quite simply seems that police have got their priorities wrong. On this question young people's impressions frequently take a very general form, as in the case of these 12 year-old boys from Broughton:

> They think you're up to something cos they've got nothing else to dae cos they dinnae do their job properly.

> They're not in the right places at the right time, they're just lazy ken, they look for wee boys and that an pick them up.

On the other hand, they can take the from of quite specific complaints, as in the case of these 13 year-old girls from Marchmont:

> They don't check local enough, like the park where we were being bullied yesterday.

> I think there should be someone sitting on the bus all the time - they sort of cause trouble at the back, older people.

> Places like the Meadows should have them *(the police)*, cos I don't like walking across there at night time. I worry about it but I do it.

The contradictions young people feel as a result of their experiences is compounded by the view that they are not listened to, or taken seriously, by either adults or the police. As one 12 year-old girl from Wester Hailes said: 'They dinnae give you a chance to talk.' The important point is that young people perceive themselves to be on the receiving end of an apparent collusion between adults and the police. As a couple of 14 year-old boys from Wester Hailes put it:

> If there was a windae bein smashed and you were near you'd get the blame for it.

> Say a windae had been smashed and there was a couple of adults in that square that didnae like you, and they phoned the police and said you smashed that windae, the police would believe them before they believed you.

Accounts such as this reinforce young people's sense of powerlessness in relation to both the police and to adults generally. Not only do they think

146

they are subject to an unjustified degree of police attention merely because of their age, but when they are, they feel that they are given little opportunity to put their side of the story, let alone have it taken seriously:

> CS: *Would you rather there was no police at all in Wester Hailes?*
> A: Nuh.
> B: No, but they should be more understandin aboot what goes on instead of pickin on people all the time. They never gie the young ones a chance to explain or anything.
>
> *(15 year-old girls, Wester Hailes)*

The feeling that they are not listened to has a far greater impact when young people have been the victim of a crime. Thus, not only can victimisation have considerable consequences for the young person at the time, but the police reaction contributes to the impression that they are indifferent to young people's problems and concerns. As we shall below, one consequence is that young people are unwilling to report their own victimisation. The two accounts that follow give an idea of the effect this can have on the young people concerned. First, a 13 year-old boy from Wester Hailes:

> I'm up toon wi one of my pals and there's three guys. They were chasing us, we ran right in front of a police car and they seen that one had a stick they seen they were going to kick us in, the police never done nothing, if anything they laughed.

The second account concerns a 13 year-old girl from Broughton who had experienced a sexual assault:

> CS: *Did you tell anybody?*
> A: I went doon the police station.
> CS: *Did he get caught?*
> A: No. They never found him. I ran doon the police station cos it was just doon the road and they got my dad over and they didnae believe me at first then when they got there they found my hairband lying on the floor.
> CS: *Was it bad when folk didn't believe you?*
> A: Uh huh. Cos when I was at the police station the lady didnae believe me and she phoned ma dad and she said we'll go up and have a look anyway and she took her torch and she was looking aboot the floor for claes and she looked over at a coloured bit and ma hairband was lying there from when I was running away fae him. And he pushed me on the floor as well.

147

> CS: *Do you think the police are unfair?*
> A: Aye, they dinnae gie you a chance to talk.

These two accounts provide an indication of one aspect of young people's experience of policing. It should, however, be placed alongside a regular diet of minor adversary contact with the police, for it is these two components - *taken together* - that are responsible for the ambivalence young people feel towards the police. This ambivalence was summed up in the following depiction of the police by a 12 year-old boy living in Broughton:

> Always there when you dinnae want them, but they're never there when you do want them.

At one level, this statement merely manifests a common cliché about the police. However, it goes to the heart of the contradictory way in which young people experience and perceive the police. The ambivalence young people feel places them in a double bind. On the one hand, they want more police to assist in making public space safe for them to enjoy. On the other, they fear that increased levels of policing will merely result in more control of their lives and curtailment of their freedom. Thus, while young people may want increased policing, they baulk at the prospect of more of the same policing. Asked whether they would like more police in their area, a number of the young people expressed this feeling as follows:

> No. They would be around all the time, stop them doing the things we want to do.
> *(14 year-old girl, Wester Hailes)*

> There might be a need for them but I don't want them here.
> *(15 year-old girl, Marchmont)*

> Nuh. Jist understandin police.
> *(15 year-old girl, Wester Hailes)*

'Cautionary tales' about the police

Talk between young people about the police frequently takes the form of 'horror stories'. These tales appear to have little relation to policing as they themselves experience it. However, in some respects, they mark out how great a distance there is between themselves and the police and exemplify what has been termed the process of 'deviancy amplification' (Young, 1974). The following story provides a graphic example of the sort of account we are referring to:

A: And if you gie them one bit of cheek they'll take you ootside and punch you in the face.

B: Aye this lassie I ken, she was pregnant and they rolled her up in a mattress and they were batterin her. And she shouted out she was pregnant and they let her go.

CS: This was the police?

B: Aye.

CS: Where was that then?

B: I don't know. It wisnae my pal it was my cousins pal. It was through in Livingston.

C: Aye they wrap up in a blanket and then batter you so you dinnae get any marks on you. *(All agree)*

A: Or they'll kick you in a place that willnae bruise.

(14 year-old girls, Wester Hailes)

On the other hand, police officers commonly construct their own folk devils. Currently, that place appears to be held by the 'casuals', who, as mentioned previously, seem to be regarded as more akin to the Mafia than the loose-knit association we described in Chapter 4. The following description given to us by a police constable working in the Southside, was repeated many times, amended to include 'military-style exercises', 'intelligence systems' and 'cell-phones':

> Somebody or some people, at a football match probably, realised the potential for causing havoc and mayhem and they formed a gang, as they did in the 50s, 60s and 70s. But the difference between the gangs of those decades and the gangs we've got just now is that they've taken it a stage further. Their administration department makes ours look amateurish. They realised that many of their members would probably end up being arrested and fined. So they started up a central fund they all contribute to which is used to pay off their fines.

The truth or falsity of such accounts is not relevant here. What counts is the way in which either 'side' views the other and acts in consequence. In such circumstances, 'a bit of cheek' or 'showing who's boss' serves only to confirm mutual stereotypes. In such a way, even trivial incidents can amplify the process.

At the same time, however, some of the stories young people tell about the police take the recognisable form of 'cautionary tales', even if they may not relate directly to personal experience. Furthermore, the anxieties and worries they express are not unfamiliar in the adult world. Take, for example, the following description of the police station given, from the bench, by Lord Cooper, at that time Lord Justice-General:

In the eyes of every ordinary citizen, the venue is a sinister one. When he stands alone in such a place confronted by several police officers [...] the dice are loaded against him. *(Chalmers v. H.M. Advocate, 1954 JC 66).*

It might be objected that this statement was made some considerable time ago, since when the law and police practice have changed. However, it would be understandable if, given their inexperience and vulnerability, young people were still to share some of Lord Cooper's concerns, for the police station compounds their sense of powerlessness with one of isolation:

A: I've even heard that in the police station, if they take you doon the police station, they might even take you in a cell and beat you up.

B: Aye I know.

JW: Has that actually happened to anyone you know?

A: Aye, well I dinnae really ken him, I ken this boy, and his pal, they were drunk right, like they were aboot sixteen, they were just like walking aboot, like, pure steaming an that, they wernae shouting abuse or anything. The police picked them up, took one doon the station, right, put him into a cell and broke his arm, they broke his nose.

JW: When was that?

A: I dinnae ken when it was, quite a long time ago, they cannae even get compensation cos there was two policemen and one him.

JW: Do you think that happens quite often?

A: It does, it happens in every station. You get tooken doon to a station you get tooken in and they beat you up.

(13 year-old boys, Wester Hailes)

In a sense, therefore, stories about police stations and police brutality (and they were very common) hold elements of the 'cautionary tale'. They communicate the message that the police station is a 'dangerous' place, to be avoided. At the same time, however, the prevalence of such stories can only reinforce the reluctance of young people to report crime and to look to the police for assistance, especially in the context of the level of adversary contact and the damage we have seen this does for their perception of the police. Nonetheless, it should be stressed that in almost all such cases, tales about the police take the form of myths:

A: I've heard of some people being beaten up.

B: A couple of lassies, ken they were on the run, for stabbing a broomie *(from Broomhouse)* or something. Ken they took her in, kept her in the night, and battered her in her cell.

JW: Did you know her?

B: Well, no personally, but I've seen, I've talked to the person.

(14 year-old boys, Wester Hailes)

As with most of the stories of police brutality this one is far removed from the first person - it is about 'someone I've talked to' - and their truth is seldom an issue. In this respect, they are also 'good stories' for the telling, and all the better if it can be claimed to have happened to someone you know. This points to a further important feature of these narratives - namely, that they circulate rapidly and extensively among young people. This brings us back to the point made earlier.

Such stories contribute further testimony to the fact that 'bad' policing has a far greater impact on young people's perceptions of the police than any positive contact they may have experienced - we were told no corresponding accounts of 'good' police practice. This relates to a general point made by Lord Scarman in his Report on the Brixton Disorders (Scarman, 1982), where he argued that stories - even rumours - of police deviance spread like wildfire through certain communities at enormous cost to the police and police effectiveness.

A similar process occurs with the narration of police 'horror' stories among young people. In the process of re-telling such stories are prone to distortion and exaggeration and, in consequence, the police are unable to fulfil their tasks - if for no other reason than they are unable to act if information about crime is not forthcoming from witnesses or victims (Kinsey *et al.*, 1986). On the other hand, from the point of view of the young people concerned, they provide a stereotype of the police, which enables them to make sense of their own mundane experiences of policing. This is not to suggest that the stereotype is an accurate one, merely that for young people it serves a purpose - albeit a negative one - both in terms of their own interests and those of the police when it comes to reporting crime.

Keeping the adult world at bay: reasons for not reporting crime

Loyalty and the 'culture of defence'

One important consequence of young people's ambivalence towards the police is their perception that the police do little or nothing to help them. This forms part of a wider perception that adults in general are indifferent to their problems. In this context, young people develop their own means for coping with crime - strategies aimed at managing the problem and reducing its impact upon their lives. As we saw in Chapter 3, one such strategy is 'hanging around' in groups as a means of self-protection. For this means of protection too work it relies upon a certain loyalty towards one's peers. This then is the first of the wider contexts in which we must place young people's low levels of reporting.

This was in fact one of the strongest and most recurrent themes of our interviews with young people. Not 'grassing' on your friends was a major reason why so little crime was reported to the police. As we saw in relation to witnessing, far fewer incidents were reported to the police where the witness knew or recognised the person concerned. Loyalty is a major reason for this:

> JW: *If you saw someone stealing a bike would you tell anyone about it?*
> A: If it's your best pal you wouldnae tell, you wouldnae want to get them into trouble.
> *(14 year-old boys, Wester Hailes)*

> If you ken them you say to your pals 'I seen so-and-so doin this', but never anybody else.
> *(15 year-old girl, Wester Hailes)*

Such loyalty is not of course peculiar to groups of young people. It is something we all feel towards our friends - even when we disagree with what they have done. But in the context of young people's experience of crime, this loyalty takes on a special significance. If group support is to work as a means of self-defence, it relies on the 'solidarity' of those it protects. To break with this is to threaten the whole basis of the strategy - and with it the personal and collective safety of all.

Such loyalty, however, is never totally unqualified. In the first place, there are always a complex set of factors to be weighed up and balanced. These can include the implications for yourself and your friends; the status of the offender; the seriousness of the offence and your attitude towards the police:

> CS: *If you saw someone breaking into a house would you tell the police?*
> A: It would depend who it was, if you ken them or no.
> B: If it was somebody's hoose that you ken and you didnae ken who it was that was doin it and you liked the person whose hoose it was I'd tell them but I wouldnae tell the police.
> A: But if it was your hoose and I didnae ken who was doin it, I would tell the police.

152

C: I would tell the person I'd seen it gettin broke into but I wouldnae tell them who it was. Cos they would obviously go to the police and then it would be me in it.
B: But if you didnae ken the person . . .
C: If I kent the person I wouldnae be telling anyway.
(15 year-old girls, Wester Hailes)

Neither does this loyalty mean that matters are left unspoken, or that nothing is done about it. Young people often have there own informal ways of expressing disapproval - including 'shunning' the person concerned:

CS: *Would you report someone breaking into to a car?*
A: It would depend if I knew them, if I knew them I'd steer clear of them and not be friends with them.
B: If I'd seen them around a lot and if I knew they wouldnae do anything to me then I'd probably say 'Hey don't do that'. But that sometimes makes things worse, like it makes them come at you. But I would report it if they carried on.
(12 year-old girls, Marchmont)

Managing the impact of crime

We argued in Chapter 3 that one of the ways in which young people learn to cope with crime is to reduce the impact it has upon their lives. Going around in groups is one strategy young people use to do this. The telling of 'cautionary tales' another. Running through both these mechanisms is the determination not to let your experience of crime dominate your life. Not reporting the things that happen to you, or the things you see happening around you, must be seen in this context. Reporting an incident of this nature is to run the risk of amplifying both its importance and its consequences. It may involve explaining it to your parents, or to the police. It might possibly take a considerable amount of effort to get yourself believed. It may even involve turning up in a court room to give evidence. All of these things run counter to the ways in which young people attempt to reduce the impact which crime has upon them. The decision whether to tell anyone is always influenced by these considerations:

A: I would go and get someone else, go and get help.
B: If I knew the person I would go in and stop it. If she was gettin battered silly I would try and get her off.
C: I think other people should help you.
B: But it happens so quickly.
A: They could have a weapon.

153

B: You never know if you go in and that if you're going to get involved and beaten up.
(15 year-old girls, Broughton)

One of the prime considerations in terms of the impact of crime, is the fear of reprisals. Though we suspect this factor is sometimes emphasised at the expense of other reasons for not reporting, it was nevertheless, a genuine concern of many of the young people we talked to. Again the point is to minimise the impact of crime. The fear of reprisals is specifically related to that of amplification, both of which are captured in the following account:

CS: *Would you tell the police if you saw somebody being mugged?*

A: No it's wrong to grass, you dinnae wanna get involved in it because you have to go down the police station and get questioned and all that and if it goes to court you couldnae handle it.

B: And if you grass you get battered about, ken if there's loads o hooligans on the muggers side.
(14 year-old girls, Wester Hailes)

While the concern about reprisals is a real one, it is often conveyed in exaggerated, almost mythical terms; again, rarely does it take the form of personal accounts. The following represent classic examples of the form that 'reprisals' stories take:

If you get found out, if you get seen talking to the police and someone gets pulled up, then its pretty obvious that it's you and you told on them and then you get duffed. And duffed and duffed and duffed. And then stabbed.
(15 year-old boy, Wester Hailes)

If they think you've grassed on them, you're likely to have a knife in you're back.
(14 year-old boy, Wester Hailes)

In many ways the fear of reprisal stories constitute another set of 'cautionary tales'. They convey particular warnings about the ways in which reporting crime can *heighten* the impact it has upon you. Again, the point is not whether such reprisals actually take place, but the fact that young people themselves believe they might. In this sense, they convey an important - if misleading - message about the likely consequences of reporting crime. Not only will the initial contact be amplified, but it might just possibly result in further victimisation.

A further way in which reporting an incident can worsen the impact upon a young people's lives is if they themselves are held to be 'responsible' in some way for its occurrence. This is the situation where reporting an incident can lead to 'double trouble' for them. Thus, not only are they victims of the crime, but telling an adult may lead to further sanctions being imposed upon them. As some 14 year-old girls in Wester Hailes explained:

> A: If anything happened to ma pals I'd never tell cos I'd never be allowed out again.
> B: Aye. That's sometimes why people dinnae tell their parents cos they jist keep them in 24 hours a day after that and they're feared to let them go out ever again.

It is clear from the above statements that losing the freedom to go out was enough to ensure some would not tell their parents about a serious incident, even though the parents would feel that they were acting in the best interests of the young person. In a similar way, their parents may try to control what friends they have if one of them seems to be a 'trouble maker'. As some 15 year-old girls from Wester Hailes explained:

> A: You dinnae tell your ma or that.
> B: She'd say 'Stay away fer them. Dinnae get into trouble.'
> C: Aye that's what mine says to me.

In such situations young people fear they will be blamed for their own victimisation either because of the people they were with or, more commonly, where they were at the time. Young people are sometimes victims in places where they have been warned not to go and by telling an adult they give this information away. Again this situation is not peculiar to young people - it is not so long since an English judge caused considerable controversy by referring to the 'contributory negligence' of a victim of a rape on the grounds that she had been hitch-hiking. Nonetheless, it is just one more instance where young people's diminished status as 'children' clearly effects the extent to which they relate their experiences of crime to the adult world.

Of course, some young people do report incidents to adults, even with this knowledge of what may be the unintended consequences. But, as has been documented in detail in relation to child abuse, it is not always easy for them to be believed. As one young person put it when asked about whether they would report a crime - 'You might only be called a liar anyway.' As we have seen in earlier chapters, even with serious offences the onus is often on the young person to prove that they are telling the truth.

155

This is one context where young people's perceptions of the police cannot be excluded from their decision whether or not to report an incident. As we saw earlier, 'not being listened to' was one of the major factors in accounting for young people's impression that the police do little to protect or assist them. In this regard, a version of 'double trouble' enters into the question of whether to report an incident to the police. Young people's past experience of the police can lead them to fear the consequences of reporting crime to them:

> They'll think you're hidin something and all that. They're no very understanding.
> *(15 year-old girl, Wester Hailes)*

> They'd give you too much hassle 'Were you involved, were you involved', trying to get you to confess or something. They'd start questioning you.
> *(15 year-old boy, Wester Hailes)*

The concern here is clearly that their point of view will be met with suspicion by the police. In this context, young people's reasons for not reporting are clearly influenced by a very specific concern about amplification. It is a fear that their initial contact with crime - whether as victim or witness - will be compounded by further 'trouble' at the hands of the police. The police's conception about the status of 'children's' evidence clearly stands in the way of young people reporting their experiences to them.

On the other hand, young people also display a more pragmatic side to their cynicism as the following comments from two boys in Wester Hailes reveal:

> There's nae use grassing, the police dinnae do anything. I mean if you get your bike chored, the police say 'Oh well we'll look into it.' Its aboot eight o'clock at night, they'll look for it fer aboot two hours or something.
> *(14 year-old boy, Wester Hailes)*

> The police never look into anything properly. If they see it *(his bike)* they'll just say 'Hey you', and they'll cycle away and that'll be it. They willnae chase them or anything.
> *(15 year-old boy, Wester Hailes)*

Such responses are deeply discouraging. For as many studies have shown, without the voluntary cooperation of members of the public and a ready flow of information between police and public, clear-up rates fall and dissatisfaction with the service rises (Chatterton, 1976; Baldwin and Kinsey,

1982). Thus, when such cynicism is taken in combination with the other reservations young people hold about contact with the police and the difficulties they experience in reporting incidents, it is difficult to see how the police can offer an effective service *for* young people. Sadly, this 14 year-old from Wester Hailes speaks for many in this regard when he says:

> The police havenae done anything for you, so why should you
> do them a favour.

Conclusion: crime, policing and adult indifference

One of the central themes of this study has been that young people have to cope with levels of contact with crime that the adult population would find intolerable. We have also seen how young people deal with their experience of crime with very little recourse to the adult world. This is especially the case with the formal institutions of the criminal justice system, such as the police. We also suspect that this is the case with regard to adults in general. Comparing the data from the Edinburgh Crime Survey (Anderson *et al.*, 1990) with the results presented here, it would seem that young people tell adults very little about the things that happen to them. Young people, it seems, perceive the adult world in general, and the police in particular, as being indifferent towards their problems. Irrespective of the accuracy of these perceptions, they have a number of consequences.

In the first place, young people are left to negotiate their problems without reference to the adult world. They develop their own strategies for coping with the realities of crime and policing. We outlined some of these in Chapter 3. A central feature of all these strategies is the attempt to reduce the impact that crime has on their everyday lives. 'Not grassing', we have argued, has to be seen in this context. To report something that happens to you is to risk exacerbating its effects on your life. Either as a victim or a witness you may be asked to explain yourself, overcome the disbelief of others, even turn up in court to give evidence. All these things inflate the importance of the initial incident. All risk giving crime a paramount place in your life and curtailing your freedom. As such they are to be avoided, if possible.

These strategies are developed in the context of young people not being taken seriously by adults or the police - or, worse still, being held in some way responsible for the problems they experience. As a result, the routine troubles that young people face are hidden from and invisible to the adult world. This in turn increases the extent of the latter's disbelief. As a result, those incidents that are bought to light are met with yet more scepticism and apparent indifference. Young people do not 'grass' because they anticipate such adult indifference and because they do not report, the incredulity increases. This is indeed a 'vicious circle' - but one whose explanation and consequences exceed the parameters of young people and the police. Its elements are set out in the diagram below.

The vicious circle of young people and crime

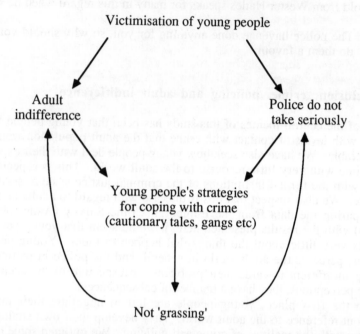

Victimisation of young people

Adult indifference

Police do not take seriously

Young people's strategies for coping with crime (cautionary tales, gangs etc)

Not 'grassing'

A major theme of this study has been that the consequences of this vicious circle are both manifest, and damaging for all concerned. The police are deprived of the information that young people undoubtedly have and that they require to successfully investigate crime. Faced with this situation, the police are left to resort to the very adversarial methods that contributed to this lack of information in the first place. Thus, within the vicious circle that characterises young people's relations with the adult world, there pertains another more specific one pertaining to their relations with the police.

More importantly, adults in general continue to be kept in the dark about the levels of contact with crime that young people experience. By refusing to take seriously their concerns, we continue to reproduce and buttress an 'innocent' conception of childhood that denies validity to young people's experiences. This is not to say that young people be given *all* the rights and responsibilities of adults. Rather, it is to argue that while we continue to treat young people as 'children' and fail to take seriously their problems and concerns, the situation we have described in this book is unlikely to improve.

It is for young people themselves, however, that the consequences are most serious. This is not to suggest that their lives are a misery, or that they are paralysed by worries and fears about crime. As we have seen, young people manage. They continue to use and enjoy the streets and other public places in spite of the dangers that such places hold.

This cannot be a reason for complacency, however. What is required is that we develop the means by which young people can continue to enjoy the freedom that 'childhood' brings, while ensuring that this enjoyment is not marred by the threat of crime and harassment. Young people may indeed learn how to cope with crime - the tragedy is that they have to. If we are to overcome this we need to break the vicious circle that we have entered. It is only by doing so that we will be able to offer a different and better future to - among others - this 15 year-old girl:

> So you jist get into trouble and the place gets a worser and worser name and your life gets more and more mucked up and that's Wester Hailes and that's the end of the story.

Bibliography

Abercrombie, P. and Plumstead, D. (1949), *A Civic Survey and Plan for the City and Royal Burgh of Edinburgh*, Edinburgh: Oliver and Boyd.

Anderson, S., Grove Smith, C., Kinsey, R. and Wood, J. (1990), *The Edinburgh Crime Survey*, The Scottish Office: Edinburgh.

Aries, P. (1962), *Centuries of Childhood*, Penguin: Harmondsworth.

Baker, K. (1990), 'Crime Culture', speech delivered to the Centre for Policy Studies Conference, London, May.

Baldwin, J. and Bottoms, A.E. (1976), *The Urban Criminal*, Tavistock: London.

Baldwin, R. and Kinsey, R. (1982), *Police Powers and Politics*, Quartet: London.

Becker, H. (1970), 'Whose Side Are We On?', in J. Douglas (ed.), *The Relevance of Sociology*, Appleton-Century-Crofts: New York.

Bordua, D. (1961), 'A Critique of Sociological Interpretations of Gang Delinquency', *Annals of the American Academy of Political and Social Science*, 338:120-136.

Bowlby, J. (1946), *Forty-Four Juvenile Thieves*, Bailliere: Tindall and Cox.

Box, S. (1981), *Deviance, Reality and Society*, Holt, Reinhardt and Winston: London.

Box, S., Hale, C. and Andrews, G. (1986), 'Fear of Crime: Causes, Consequences and Control', Applied Statistics Research Department, University of Kent: Canterbury.

Brunvand, J.H. (1983), *The Vanishing Hitchhiker: Urban Legends and Their Meanings*, Picador: London.

Chambers, G. and Millar, A. (1983), *Investigating Sexual Assault*, The Scottish Office: Edinburgh.

Chambers, G. and Tombs, J. (1984), *The British Crime Survey (Scotland)*, The Scottish Office: Edinburgh.

Chatterton, M. (1976), 'Police in Social Control', in King, J.F.S. (ed.), *Control Without Custody*, CUP: Cambridge.

160

Cloward, R. and Ohlin, L. (1960), *Delinquency and Opportunity*, Free Press: New York.

Cohen, A. (1955), *Delinquent Boys*, Free Press: Glencoe.

Crawford, A., Lea, J., Woodhouse, T. and Young, J. (1990), *Second Islington Crime Survey*, Middlesex Polytechnic: Centre for Criminology.

Damer, S. (1989), *From Moorepark to 'Wine Alley'*, Edinburgh University Press: Edinburgh.

Farson, R. (1978), *Birthrights*, Penguin: Harmondsworth.

Freeman, M. (1983), *The Rights and Wrongs of Children*, Pinter: London.

Garner, K. (1989), *Does Deprivation Damage?*, Centre for Educational Sociology: University of Edinburgh.

Gillis, J. (1974), *Youth and History*, Academic Press: London.

Grimshaw, R. and Jefferson, T. (1987), *Interpreting Police Work*, Unwin Hyman: London.

Hague, C. (1984), *The Development of Planning Thought*, Hutchinson: London.

Hall, S. and Jefferson, T. (eds.), (1976), *Resistance Through Rituals*, Hutchinson: London.

Heydon, J.D. (1984), *Cases and Materials on Evidence*, Butterworths: London.

Holt, J. (1975), *Escape from Childhood*, Penguin: Harmondsworth.

Home Office (1989), *Report to the Working Group on Fear of Crime (the Grade Report)*, HMSO: London.

Hough, M. and Mayhew, P. (1983), *The British Crime Survey (England and Wales)*, HMSO: London.

Jones, T., Maclean, B. and Young, J. (1986), *The Islington Crime Survey*, Gower: Aldershot.

Kinsey, R. (1985), *First Report of the Merseyside Crime Survey*, Merseyside County Council: Liverpool.

Kinsey, R., Lea, J., and Young, J. (1986), *Losing the Fight Against Crime*, Blackwells: Oxford.

Kinsey, R. and Loader, I. (1990), 'The Myth of the Mindless Hooligan', *Scotland on Sunday*, 14 January.

Kinsey, R. (1992), *Policing the City*, The Scottish Office: Edinburgh.

Kinsey, R. and Anderson, S. (1992), *Crime and the Quality of Life - Public Perceptions and Experiences of Crime: Findings from the 1988 British Crime Survey (Scotland)*, The Scottish Office: Edinburgh.

Loader, I. (1993), *Youth, Policing and Democratic Accountability*, Ph.D. thesis: University of Edinburgh.

Lothian Regional Council (1988a), *Poverty in Edinburgh*, Lothian Regional Council: Edinburgh.

Lothian Regional Council (1988b), *Shopping Survey*, Lothian Regional Council: Edinburgh.

McCrone, D. and Elliot, B. (1989), *Power and Property in the City*, Edinburgh University Press: Edinburgh.

Manning, P. (1977), *Police Work*, Camb.: MIT Press: Mass.

Matza, D. (1964), *Delinquency and Drift*, Wiley: New York.

Maxfield, M. (1984), *Fear of Crime in England and Wales*, HMSO: London.

Maxfield, M. (1988), *Explaining Fear of Crime*, HMSO: London.

Morgan, J. and Zedner, L. (1992), *Child Victims: Crime, Impact and Criminal Justice*, Clarendon: Oxford.

Muncie, J. (1984), *The Trouble with Kids Today*, Open University Press: Milton Keynes.

Murray, C. (1984), *Losing Ground*, Basic Books: New York.

Murray, C. (1990), *The Emerging British Underclass*, IEA: London.

Piaget, J. (1983), *The Moral Judgement of the Child*, Penguin: Harmondsworth.

Reiner, R. (1978), *The Blue-Coated Worker*, CUP: Cambridge.

Scarman, L. (1982), *The Scarman Report*, Penguin: Harmondsworth.

Schur, E. (1965), *Radical Non-Intervention*, Prentice-Hall: Eaglewood Cliff, N.J.

Shapland, J. and Vagg, J. (1988), *Policing by the Public*, Routledge: London.

Sparks, J.R. (1992), 'Reason and Unreason in "Left Realism": Some Problems in the Construction of Fear of Crime', in Matthews, R. and Young, J. (eds.), *Issues in Realist Criminology*, Sage: London.

Sparks, R.F., Genn, H. and Dodd, D. (1977), *Surveying Victims*, Wiley: London.

Spencer, D. and Flinn, R. (1990), *The Evidence of Children*, Blackstone: London.

Wilson, W.J. (1987), *The Truly Disadvantaged*, University of Chicago Press: Chicago.

Young, J. (1971), 'The Role of the Police as Amplifiers of Deviancy' in Cohen, S. (ed.) *Images of Deviance*, Penguin: Harmondsworth.